MICROCOMPUTERS IN EDUCATION

THE ELLIS HORWOOD SERIES IN COMPUTERS AND THEIR APPLICATIONS

Series Editor: BRIAN MEEK
Director of the Computer Unit, Queen Elizabeth College, University of London

The series aims to provide up-to-date and readable texts on the theory and practice of computing, with particular though not exclusive emphasis on computer applications. Preference is given in planning the series to new or developing areas, or to new approaches in established areas.

The books will usually be at the level of introductory or advanced undergraduate courses. In most cases they will be suitable as course texts, with their use in industrial and commercial fields always kept in mind. Together they will provide a valuable nucleus for a computing science library.

INTERACTIVE COMPUTER GRAPHICS IN SCIENCE TEACHING
Edited by J. McKENZIE, University College, London, L. ELTON, University of Surrey, R. LEWIS, Chelsea College, London.

INTRODUCTORY ALGOL 68 PROGRAMMING
D. F. BRAILSFORD and A. N. WALKER, University of Nottingham.

GUIDE TO GOOD PROGRAMMING PRACTICE
Edited by B. L. MEEK, Queen Elizabeth College, London and P. HEATH, Plymouth Polytechnic.

CLUSTER ANALYSIS ALGORITHMS: For Data Reduction and Classification of Objects
H. SPÄTH, Professor of Mathematics, Oldenburg University.

DYNAMIC REGRESSION: Theory and Algorithms
L. J. SLATER, Department of Applied Engineering, Cambridge University and H. M. PESARAN, Trinity College, Cambridge

FOUNDATIONS OF PROGRAMMING WITH PASCAL
LAWRIE MOORE, Birkbeck College, London.

PROGRAMMING LANGUAGE STANDARDISATION
Edited by B. L. MEEK, Queen Elizabeth College, London and I. D. HILL, Clinical Research Centre, Harrow.

THE DARTMOUTH TIME SHARING SYSTEM
G. M. BULL, The Hatfield Polytechnic

RECURSIVE FUNCTIONS IN COMPUTER SCIENCE
R. PETER, formerly Eötvos Lorand University of Budapest.

FUNDAMENTALS OF COMPUTER LOGIC
D. HUTCHISON, University of Strathclyde.

THE MICROCHIP AS AN APPROPRIATE TECHNOLOGY
Dr. A. BURNS, The Computing Laboratory, Bradford University

SYSTEMS ANALYSIS AND DESIGN FOR COMPUTER APPLICATION
D. MILLINGTON, University of Strathclyde.

COMPUTING USING BASIC: An Interactive Approach
TONIA COPE, Oxford University Computing Teaching Centre.

RECURSIVE DESCENT COMPILING
A. J. T. DAVIE and R. MORRISON, University of St. Andrews, Scotland.

PASCAL IMPLEMENTATION
M. DANIELS and S. PEMBERTON, Brighton Polytechnic.

SOFTWARE ENGINEERING
K. GEWALD, G. HAAKE, and W. PFADLER, Siemens AG, Munich

AN INTRODUCTION TO PROGRAMMING LANGUAGE TRANSITION
R. E. BERRY, University of Lancaster

ADA: A PROGRAMMER'S CONVERSION COURSE
M. J. STRATFORD-COLLINS, U.S.A.

MICROCOMPUTERS IN EDUCATION

Editor:

I. C. H. SMITH, B. Sc., M.Sc., Ph.D.
Department of Physiology
Queen Elizabeth College, University of London

ELLIS HORWOOD LIMITED
Publishers · Chichester

Halsted Press: a division of
JOHN WILEY & SONS
New York · Brisbane · Chichester · Toronto

42720

First published in 1982
Reprinted 1982

ELLIS HORWOOD LIMITED
Market Cross House, Cooper Street, Chichester, West Sussex, PO19 1EB, England

The publisher's colophon is reproduced from James Gillison's drawing of the ancient Market Cross, Chichester.

Distributors:

Australia, New Zealand, South-east Asia:
Jacaranda-Wiley Ltd., Jacaranda Press,
JOHN WILEY & SONS INC.,
G.P.O. Box 859, Brisbane, Queensland 40001, Australia

Canada:
JOHN WILEY & SONS CANADA LIMITED
22 Worcester Road, Rexdale, Ontario, Canada.

Europe, Africa:
JOHN WILEY & SONS LIMITED
Baffins Lane, Chichester, West Sussex, England.

North and South America and the rest of the world:
Halsted Press: a division of
JOHN WILEY & SONS
605 Third Avenue, New York, N.Y. 10016, U.S.A.

© 1982 C. Smith/Ellis Horwood Limited

Smith, I. C. H.
Microcomputers in education. –
(Ellis Horwood series in computers and their applications)
1. Computer-assisted instruction – Congresses
2. PET (Computer) – Congresses
I. Title
371.3'9445   LB 1026.46

ISBN 0-85312-424-8 (Ellis Horwood Ltd. – Library Edn.)
ISBN 0-470-27319-4 (Halsted Press – Library Edn.)
ISBN 0-85312-538-4 (Ellis Horwood Ltd. – Student Edn.)
ISBN 0-470-27362-3 (Halsted Press – Paperback Edn.)

Typeset in Press Roman by Ellis Horwood Ltd.
Printed in Great Britain by R. J. Acford, Chichester.

Table of Contents

PART I – THE DEVELOPMENT OF COMPUTER ASSISTED LEARNING

Chapter 1 A systems approach to curriculum development,
the Manchester project for computer studies in schools
Kathleen Hennessy, Lecturer in Systems Analysis,
University of Manchester Institute of Science and Technology

Chapter 2 Mechanism for CAL origination
Bob Lewis, St. Martin's College, Lancaster

PART 2 – LANGUAGES FOR MICROCOMPUTERS IN EDUCATION

Table of Contents

Chapter 17 School administration without discs: how much can be done?
Ian Birnbaum, Ramsey Abbey School, Huntingdon

Foreword

Ten years ago, the idea of having a self-standing computer in a school classroom seemed a science fiction dream. At that time, a terminal connected to the county treasurer's office was the best that many could visualise, and in several cases all that could be used were travelling terminals that appeared in the school for two months at a time. Now we have a microcomputer in the classroom, totally under the control of teacher and pupil, and by the end of next year, every secondary school will have at least one and many will have more. It is with great pleasure therefore that I take this opportunity to write in this publication, the report of the first PET conference, more especially as the PET was the computer that was really at the beginning of this revolutionary change in our schools.

That this development is important for the future of education is clear from the government support given to the Microelectronics Education Programme as an initiative to increase the use and understanding of this new technology. As is now well known, the Programme is concerned with distributing information and software, stimulating and guiding teacher training and initiating curriculum development activities. The scope of the Programme's work is broader than just a consideration of computing alone, but this will form a solid core of the work being undertaken.

One of the emphases of the Programme is to ensure a comprehensive approach to the use of the computer. It is not just a machine for use in Computer Studies in the school, but can be of considerable value in a wide range of subjects. Perhaps the one that springs first to mind is its use in helping children learn more effectively in all the central disciplines of the curriculum through the use of specially designed programs. This computer aided learning is now at the heart of a great deal of activity in the preparation of appropriate software, and further experiment and development is required in order to define clearly the parameters of the most effective programs. Nevertheless, it is one of the most important uses of the computer in the classroom, and has the additional benefit of giving children a familiarity with the device.

For those involved in science and technology, there are further uses of the equipment which need to be exploited at the heart of these curricula. Linking the equipment to scientific experiments which it can control or monitor gives an insight into the use of computers in industrial and commercial situations as well as leading to activities and calculations which would have been impossible without it. In technology studies, the computer can be further used to invest project designs with a sense of commercial and industrial reality which is economically essential to the future well-being of society.

Chapters on all these topics, including real classroom activities that practising teachers actually use, are included in this book, and it is important that these should be seen as central to any study of the use of the computer. It is inevitable that a conference report should also be concerned with the arguments concerning the mechanics of the computer and its languages. The trend towards increasing structure in BASIC is illustrated by the chapters on COMAL, and the arguments about the relative values of each will continue to be aired. No language can become a national standard at this time, but it is necessary to identify and foster the trends which respond to the needs of teachers.

At the centre of the revolution produced by the new technology is the treatment of information. The retrieval and manipulation of data is the essential facility of the computer, and it is also much of the substance of current education. In learning to cope with the effects of the new technology, it is necessary for children to understand the characteristics of information and explore the different means of storing and retrieving it. This means that we need to encourage children to use the computer and databases for project work and learn how to use the information they gain.

It is easy to allow the excitement of manipulating the equipment to get in the way of learning, for studies of the machine itself to be a more significant end than the general curriculum. Of all the dangers facing the school response to the new technology, this is probably the most threatening. It is important for teachers to see the computer as a tool, a valuable weapon in the armoury of instruments at their disposal to help them encourage children to learn. For the majority of children, the reason for the computer in school is certainly not Computer Studies, but it is to aid familiarity with using a tool like this for the process of learning as part of everyday life.

But the technology is not standing still. Networking microcomputers within a school gives more children more opportunities to use the equipment, and linking them to mainframes, viewdata and other databases provides access to large reservoirs of programs and information. This is what is happening in the commercial and domestic world, and the education system must respond.

This book covers all this ground with chapters by exponents of the different activities in this country. We have already come a long way since the first PET entered the classroom, but we must continue to retain the goal of responding to the real learning needs of children.

Richard Fothergill
Director, Microelectronics Education Programme

Introduction

Computers have had a firm role in education for decades, yet in the last three years there has been something unique about the effects of microcomputers. It is not the increased scale of use nor their immediacy of response (which are but consequences of decreased hardware costs) it is simply that microcomputers have made us all into computer managers as well as users. The freedoms of having one's own computer are well known; the obligations frequently forgotten. Thus it is with no apology that most of the articles in this book are concerned with what are essentially management problems. Perhaps the first such problem is what language to use. Two papers here argue strongly for COMAL. We have yet to see if this language is adopted or if BASIC is progressively adapted to include COMAL-like instructions such as in currently available PET ROM variants and by concealed line numbering. The choice of the user-cum-manager is important.

The revolution is thus not in microelectronics but in personal computer systems of which the Commodore PET is the archetype. The 1979 national conference on computer assisted learning was perhaps the apogee for terminal-based educational systems but it was there that my 8k PET was rewarded with the remark, 'Keep it for prosperity, you've a Model T there'. And so it proved to be; they have sold in hundreds of thousands, are available for any language provided its BASIC, and are reliable. However most of the articles here are not simply about PETs but about computers where the user is in charge of the system.

Commodore have changed the name on the front of their machines enough times to make it worth recalling that PET stands for 'Personal Electronic Transactor' – a sure way to remind us that what we have bought is simply a device for routing electrical signals. Its use is our problem and, as I am sure this conference shows, also our success. One person deserves special mention, Nick Green, the 'special effects' man of Commodore UK. His specification of PETNET in this book belies his desire for the provision of information exchange as being a key to progress in our society. It is his enthusiasm that led to this conference and we are indebted to him and Commodore for their substantial contribution and support.

I.C.H.S.

CHAPTER 1

A systems approach to curriculum development, the Manchester project for computer studies in schools

Kathleen Hennessy, Lecturer in System Analysis,
University of Manchester Institute of Science and Technology

When people first look at schools computing, it seems a fairly easy task: you get some textbooks, you get a microcomputer, and you get a teacher and away you go. Those who have been in the game a little longer say computer studies is more difficult to teach successfully than most other subjects. For one thing, computer studies is a moving target; it is changing rapidly with the development of computer technology every year. It also involves far-reaching effects and influences which distort and confuse the situation.

In the process of establishing a specification for the provision of computing facilities for schools computing, the currently-used concepts and techniques of curriculum development and systems analysis were not up to the task. Until new approaches were used, it was not possible to obtain realistic results that actually worked in the school classroom.

1.1 CURRICULUM DEVELOPMENT AND SYSTEMS ANALYSIS

In order to be able to use a curriculum development method that works, we need to find one that is able to achieve the performance established as the basic design objective. This inevitably means actual performance *in the classroom.* In all the literature on curriculum development, there is no instance of a secondary school curriculum design which, when evaluated in strict performance terms, has met original requirements. In many cases there were no specific performance standards established at any point; in others, they related to the internal workings of the curriculum development rather than its impact in the classroom. [1]

The woolliness of thinking in this area is exemplified by Michael Eraut's three stages of curriculum development in the context of technology in education:

(1) Formulating aims.
(2) Selecting objectives in accordance with the aims.
(3) Developing the means of achieving the objectives. [2]

When Philip Halsey was principal of secondary development projects at the Schools Council he described the process by which the Schools Mathematics Project was carried out: 'By dealing simultaneously with teaching materials, the teachers, syllabuses and examinations, the innovation process is much more likely to be successful'. [3] He stressed the importance of trying out materials in schools and getting feedback from teachers, but at no point did his thinking move toward getting a realistic 'fit' of the innovation into the classroom processes. The chaos that ensues from these approaches is portrayed in detail in Gross and Giaquinta's study of a curriculum innovation project.[4]

Because systems analysis has much more of a scientific background, and has been used in large on-line commercial computer system developments that have been successfully implemented, it was used to attempt to implement system designs into the computing classroom system. At first, well-established methods were used: IBM's Study Organization Plan (SOP) [5], which is based on the concept of a system as

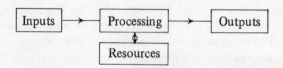

In 1974–6, several attempts were made to develop a workable system of provision for secondary school computer studies using SOP. Although the method has a number of very useful features, including very precise definition of time constraints, it still resulted in an unworkable design. The Digilog computer terminal was used; with its built-in acoustic coupler and its connections for magnetic tape cassette recording and its television link, it fitted well within the design constraints that emerged from the SOP model. It soon became obvious when the facilities were tried out, however, that the school's television set was not always available when needed, nor could it be carried up two flights of stairs to the scheduled classroom. A further look at current systems analysis methods and the resulting working systems in commerce and industry revealed that many systems operate in a makeshift fashion having in many cases departed radically from the original design in order to produce usable results. Other much-publicised new systems had been discontinued completely. So much for the science of systems analysis!

1.2 WIDER SYSTEMS THAT AFFECT CURRICULUM DEVELOPMENT

Curriculum development as a process can be seen to involve several systems that operate at different levels, carrying out different functions in particular time frames in their own specific environmental settings which gives each its own set of priorities:

- the 11–16 statutory supervision system:
- the qualifications-granting system for 16+ pupils;
- the materials preparation system;
- the equipment and materials supply system;
- the subject and technology system.

It is important to keep in mind that each of these systems interacts in its own way with the other systems, and that each system has its own 'survival imperative' and ways of adapting to its environment and managing its internal affairs. Any curriculum innovation that disrupts these patterns either cannot achieve an enduring impact on the systems or will affect the performance of the systems to the extent that their survival prospects are affected. Thus any attempt to achieve a lasting change in a school curriculum has to take into account the characteristics of each affected system, and to incorporate features that will enable each of these systems to cope with the change.

The 11–16 statutory supervision system

Although throughout the literature, the system which involves compulsory attendance at school by children from the ages of 11 to 16 is called *secondary education,* evidence from school records and correspondence, from local education authority bulletins and circulars, and from local press reports indicates that the main priority is the supervision of children between 11 and 16 who are required by law to be present at school. Whether they are educated there or not is of secondary importance, as can be seen from any school punishment book, detention register and the need for conformity of dress, appearance and behaviour.

The system carries out many other activities outside the purely education role: catering, travel, sports, hobbies and crafts, welfare, community and charity work, etc. Time is divided into time slots of identical length and each day has the same number of time slots. Children are assigned to class groups, to which they normally belong for at least one academic year. Each class group is assigned a class room and a class teacher to supervise the pupils in the group, for each time slot in the day. This schedule or timetable is rigidly followed, the priority being not to leave a class group unsupervised. The system has the same structure, pattern of working relationships, and rigid time constraints that are found in industrial batch production systems.

There is no evidence that curriculum design and development activities form part of the normal working pattern of any secondary school teacher, deputy head, heads of departments, or headmaster in any of the 22 schools studied. When these activities are carried out by teachers, it is during summer or other holidays, in the evenings, or on secondment from teaching duties, and often in the face of considerable opposition on the part of senior members of staff. Curriculum innovation takes place as a result of the 11-16 statutory supervision system's interaction with other systems in its environment, rather than from within.

The 16+ qualifications-granting system

The statutory system normally purchases assessment services from one or more of examining boards, whereby teachers submit pupils' course work and/or scripts written by the pupils during specified periods of time on specific dates according to an examination paper provided by the board. Marks awarded by external examiners are given considerable importance by the teacher's colleagues, the pupils' employers, and the pupils' parents, as well as the heads of department, deputy head, headmaster and advisers or inspectors. These results are seen as a major measure of performance of an individual school, and in particular of an individual teacher.

In general, those curriculum innovations which find their way into examination board syllabi, onto examination papers, and into assessment guidelines, tend to be seen in pupils' notebooks and to be presented in class. On the other hand, those innovations carried out by teachers either on their own or in small local groups do not have lasting impact unless they are adopted by the examination boards.[6] The same applies to those innovations carried out by larger regional and national projects: they tend to disappear without trace or to emerge in some other form if they are not included in formal examination syllabi.

The time scale for adoption of material by examination boards covers at least three years, and usually much longer. In the fast-changing computer scene, this means that most examination syllabi are seriously out of date. To some extent, examiners accommodate this problem by setting questions that reflect recent developments; but this cannot be done to any great extent because the syllabi form the basis of the material presented to pupils who are studying for the examinations.

The materials preparation system

Preparation of materials for use in the presentation of information and development of skills and concepts among children 11-16 years of age takes four forms:

The teacher, working alone or in consulation with outside people, prepares his/her own teaching materials. These are frequently *ad hoc,* rarely evaluated, and usually done by the teacher in his/her own time; they frequently contain errors of fact or concept and emphasis among topics is often very uneven. In general, these materials tend to present topics that can be quickly mastered and which generate large amounts of 'seat work', such as programming and flowcharting.

Local groups of teachers, usually cooperating to run a Certificate of Secondary Education Mode III (own syllabus and assessment) programme, also prepare materials for joint use. In some cases, these materials form the basis for curriculum innovation that can be found in examination board syllabi, but in general their lasting impact on the curriculum is minimal.

Publication of materials prepared by teachers or groups of teachers has a significant impact on what is taught in the classroom. An example of this is the ICL-CES series, which covers from 20% – 50% of CSE and O-level syllabi. Books in the series are used extensively because their format allows teachers who know nothing about the subject of computing to assign reading and questions to be answered and written in pupils' notebooks. Thus the teacher can plan most of the computer studies lessons around the series. In most of the schools visited, these texts were the main or only source of material on computing to which the teachers and pupils had regular access; often the rest of the official syllabus was ignored because material was too difficult to put together in the time available. The timescale for publication of materials was usually between two and three years.

Regional and national schemes, such as those sponsored by the Schools Council, the Nuffield Foundation, and the National Foundation for Educational Research on the national scale and the Berkshire and Hatfield projects on a regional basis, have consumed millions of pounds of public funds for curriculum development in the past decade. The impact of these projects, several years after their 'successful' conclusion, was difficult to find anywhere in the schools visited. Some traces of the Schools Mathematics Project could be seen, but the materials could not be used without extensive supplementary material to be prepared by teachers; in the end, the teachers' materials replaced the published texts. Other projects, such as the Chelsea Science Simulation scheme and the CALUSG computer-based geography project cannot be seen in most schools. Their time-scale is about the same as that of other published materials: three to five years.

There are usually considerable political and other pressures on these regional and national project groups; their priorities do not include adoption by schools, although trying out the materials in schools does seem to be important. Standards for evaluation of materials are ill-defined.

In general, the materials prepared without the aid of professional publishers tend to be ill-suited to classroom use. Teachers in general have no training and little experience in curriculum development techniques, nor do they have training or experience in designing and writing reliable computer programs. A general rule-of-thumb for development of computer-related teaching materials is about 100 man-hours for one hour of taught lesson material.[7]

The equipment and materials supply system

By far the greatest constraint on the suppliers of equipment and materials to the school system is that the total amount of money available ranges from £64 to £23 per pupil per year, with an average of £31.[8] Presuming that most pupils take eight subjects, this means £4 per subject or approximately $2\frac{1}{2}$p per lesson per pupil.

Thus the supply of microcomputer equipment to schools has to be provided completely outside the normal estimates; the Government has acknowledged this by offering a subsidy of 50% on the purchase of two British-made microcomputers. Of course, this still does not solve the problem — especially as the school's contribution to the purchase of a Research Machines 380Z would require all the funds for computer studies for more than 200 pupils. Development of computer technology and the manufacturing techniques and distribution approach over the past three years has been breathtakingly quick. The present state of the computer equipment and materials market is such that schools, with extremely limited funds, have to compete with private industry for whom £1 spent on a microcomputer is 52p saved from the taxman. Thus a £1500 configuration only costs a firm £720 in 'real' money.

Like any consumer product, the microcomputer is going through the usual stages of product distribution: pioneering, acceptance, turbulence, saturation, and obsolesence. Having just reached the end of the acceptance stage (in which there is frequent leapfrogging of products as their basic design is refined), the microcomputer is entering the turbulence stage in which marginal producers are 'shaken out' of the market and only the market leader and a few others remain. Brand preferences become important at this stage, and prices reflect cut-throat competition. Manufacturers rely heavily on dealers and distributors, and only those with well-established dealer/distribution networks survive into the saturation stage.

In this rapidly-changing situation, curriculum development (with its normal timescale of three to five years) has to be based on the facilities offered by the market leader and the main brand leaders in the field.

Classroom teaching materials have to be designed to be used in the classroom easily and on commonly-available equipment. They have to be presented in such a way and distributed so that they gain acceptance by the decision-makers in the 11–16 statutory supervision system. In general, educational publishers have the most experience and expertise in this area. Priorities are determined by the stage of the products's market development and by the profit potential of the product.

The subject and technology system

Most secondary school timetables are based on four factors: the subject, the time slot, the teacher, and the class group. The qualifications-granting system, which has a known influence on the curriculum, is based on three factors: the subject, the level of work, and the type of assessment. The common factor is the subject, and therefore we have to look at the ways in which changes are introduced into it. There is a gradual evolutionary process by which change in any subject occurs as a result of increased experience and insight over the years. But, especially in the field of computing, there are major shifts which occur with breathtaking speed. The subject of computing as taught in universities is changing rapidly, and the application of this knowledge in commerce and industry is also undergoing extensive change.

With the 'micro revolution' has come a different emphasis and approach toward information-handling techniques. Two main factors have produced the change: low cost and small size. Underlying these factors is the application of experience gained over the past generation of computer use: dialogue design, file structure and information-retrieval techniques, and information collection and dissemination.

This change can be seen in the subject of computing as it is taught in universities and, to some extent, in the way computers are used in industry. But there is little evidence of these changes in the subject syllabi of the examination boards, in which there is still a heavy emphasis on flowcharting and programming. Despite this, some of these changes are found in the classroom. Few direct links between the subject of computing or its applied technology and what was presented in the classroom could be found, however.

As part of the Manchester project, several schools were given materials and literature on the new topics; although a few interested pupils perused the material on their own, it was not presented in the classroom by the teachers. Only four teachers were found whose competence in computing could be compared with the level of the NCC Threshhold Scheme, and only one had industrial experience in the use of computers.

1.3 THE REALITIES OF THE CLASSROOM SITUATION

The activities carried out in a classroom in a secondary school during school hours are the focus of curriculum innovation efforts. These activities are tightly constrained by time slots or periods, signalled by bells. The active units in the system are the teacher and the pupils in the class group. The teacher normally is assigned to take the class group for several periods each week, to take responsibility for a specific subject such as mathematics or computer studies. The usual amount of time for computer studies is between 105 and 180 minutes per week.

The reality of the classroom situation in which 30 pupils have to share one microcomputer is light-years away from the one-child-per-keyboard situation for which most computer-based teaching materials have been designed. The influence of the 11-16 statutory supervision system, in which the class contact process occurs, shows up in the priorities of the classroom teaching situation. The first priority in the classroom, as in the school as a whole, is to keep order, without which learning activity cannot take place. Teachers frequently resort to threats and physical violence when order is threatened, and they do not use curriculum materials or methods that disrupt classroom order. Order is the 'survival imperative' of the classroom; the first criterion of any curriculum innovation therefore is that it must preserve the teacher's control over the class group. Many classroom teachers achieve control by assigning large amounts of 'seat work' — copying from the blackboard or texts into pupils' notebooks — that each pupil does at his desk on his own; it is then fairly easy to spot incipient disorder because the culprit(s) can be seen not to be writing in their exercise books.

The teacher's preparation for a lesson ranges from none to about 30 minutes. The average time reported by teachers interviewed over eight years was just under 12 minutes per lesson; with up to eight lessons a day, this means two hours' work in addition to marking and other administration jobs.

Although all classrooms have lighting and at least one electric outlet, heating is not always available; temperature ranges from $49°F$ to $81°F$ were recorded over the eight years of visits to schools in the Manchester area. All classrooms visited had enough chairs for the class group, but about 5% did not have enough tables or desks. There is almost always a teacher's desk or table in the classroom, but over 25% of classrooms have no cupboards for storage of equipment and materials.

No more than 15% of the teacher's time is spent in direct interaction with the class group; the average is less than 10%. Many teachers use the class lesson time to mark exercise books and prepare other lessons. A few teachers spend the 'seat work' time circulating around the classroom working with individual pupils, but in most cases teachers stay at the front of the room dealing with classroom administration and keeping order.

Children's attention span times varied from 2 to 30 minutes, affected by the nature of the task, distractions, and whether the work was repetitive or beyond the pupil's capacity or understanding.

Use of equipment usually involved moving the microcomputer from another classroom or secure storage area to the classroom, setting up the equipment, and getting it working. Running programs other than pupils' own work was not normally done; the few programs that were run for pupils required the teacher's constant attention and intervention. With about 120 minutes per week usually scheduled for computer studies lessons, and at least 30 minutes for set-up and classroom activities other than machine use, the maximum amount of time each pupil could have on the class's single microcomputer was 3 minutes. With a typing speed of about 15 characters per minute, this means that most pupils were able to key in about 45 characters per week.

1.4 SPECIFIC CONSTRAINTS ON CURRICULUM DEVELOPMENT

The process of carrying out curriculum innovation involves establishing another system whose specific aims are the development and implementation of the innovation. It is a separate system from those described above, with its own life span, objectives, survival imperatives, processes and resources. This system necessarily interacts with the other systems; to achieve its objectives, it must interact in a way that allows the other systems to continue to carry out their functions and remain viable.

The introduction of new material into the curriculum can take place on an evolutionary basis as the material 'seeps' into the curriculum from the surrounding environment. This process normally takes about 20 years.[9] To *engineer* a curriculum change that actually becomes a part of the fabric of the curriculum, the innovation system has to develop a strategy for interaction based on the realities of the situation, rather than on what might or ought to happen. Some of the realities that have to be faced in order to implement a lasting change are:

- the teacher is not primarily engaged in teaching; his priorities include keeping order and managing classroom activity;
- the teacher cannot prepare teaching materials due to lack of training and experience, lack of time, and lack knowledge of computing;
- examination syllabi and class materials are the main ways in which lasting change enters the school curriculum;
- in general, if material is available which can be used by pupils and does not involve preparation or effort on the part of the teacher, it is more likely to be used than material that requires preparation by the teacher;
- the maximum cost of teaching materials is $2\frac{1}{2}$p per pupil per lesson;
- each pupil has a maximum of 3 minutes per week access to a single microcomputer in the classroom;
- 'seat work' and other order-keeping activities have to form the basis of classroom teaching approach;
- curriculum topics have to be introduced on a timescale that is compatible with covering the examination syllabus;
- in general, a curriculum innovation must solve decisionmakers' problems rather than pose them, and it must be presented in this way;
- curriculum materials have to be comprehensible to the lower ability ranges in mixed-ability classes, and yet provide challenge for children in the upper ability bands;
- curriculum innovation is more likely to take place if the materials are published commercially;
- use of a computer keyboard is limited to a maximum of 45 key depressions per week per pupil;
- materials have to be used by pupils, not teachers, and should either equip them to answer examination questions or provide the basis for assessed work;
- computer equipment must have local dealer support for repairs, maintenance and technical information;
- for each hour classroom activity, 100 man-hours have to be allocated to prepare materials;

- preparation of computer programs requires training and experience in programming at least to the level of the NCC Threshold Scheme, well beyond the competence of most teachers.

Developing a strategy for a curriculum innovation system within these constraints involves understanding the nature and structure of systems in a way that stretches our present knowledge and understanding in the field of systems analysis.

1.5 SYSTEMS APPROACH FOR THE MANCHESTER PROJECT

Rather than attempt to intervene in the classroom processes as a 'hard' engineering task, a new approach was tried, whereby the structure and functions of the innovation process were seen as a system in their own right: a system that was involved in achieving a technique for the insertion of change into the classroom teaching content in a way that would endure.

System functions: a checklist

Further study of systems techniques and concepts and observation of viable systems at work showed that a viable system carries out specific functions, and that each system has one or more 'survival imperatives' which assume priority over other factors. The functions all systems seem to have in common are:

(1) *Interface* between the environment, or the rest of the universe, and the inner system, which controls the flow of materials, information and other things in and out of the system;

(2) *Storage* until required of materials, equipment, and supplies;

(3) *Transformation* of things coming into the system into things to be sent out of the system;

(4) *Transport and support* of other activities, such as cleaning and maintenance, moving materials and equipment to places where they are needed;

(5) *Coordination and control,* to manage the operation of the system: to allocate tasks and resources, and to monitor performance.

This is a summarised version of Miller's 17 system functions.[10]

Systems, people and resources

But systems activity is not carried out in a vacuum or just in concept; in reality, a system can only be perceived in terms of the way in which it marshalls people and objects to carry out functions. The physical things over which a system exerts direct influence are sometimes called its resources; they tend to have varying time imperatives: short-term, medium-term and long-term (for example, electricity, exercise books, and desks respectively).

Systems usually rely on a working unit, which assumes different character-istics depending on where it is found in the system and what functions it has to perform. In terms of most human activity systems, this unit is either a person or group of persons. For example, the working unit in the 11-16 statutory attendance system is the class group, not the pupil.

A system is also characterised by a flow or throughput of energy and things to and from its immediate environment. Many of these flows are circular and time-dependent; that is, if the system's outflow changes, its input is affected within a specific length of time (for example, if a firm fails to send out invoices, its incoming cash will be reduced 30 days later).

Interfacing with Manchester systems

Establishing a curriculum innovation system for computer studies in Manchester schools involved the establishment of working relationships among those people whose efforts skills and knowledge were needed to transform the system elements and throughput into usable curriculum materials.

Links were required to each of the systems that affect the curriculum content as presented in the classroom:

- 11-16 statutory supervision
- 16+ qualifications-granting
- materials preparation
- equipment and materials supply
- subject and technology.

An important factor in curriculum innovation was the forging of these links.

Contacts were made with the local authority advisers, headmasters and class teachers; from these contacts, a group of four Manchester teachers and the computing liaison officer for Manchester schools agreed to work together to develop curriculum materials for computer studies. At this point, it was necessary to provide a clear demarcation of the scope of the project:

(1) the main purpose was to introduce material about computer applications, which was part of the CSE and O-level computer studies syllabuses and was a topic which was not adequately covered by existing texts;

(2) the equipment to be used was the Commodore PET, which was the main microcomputer available in Manchester schools;

(3) the 'missing link' between subject/technology and teacher would be achieved as it had been with 'Fletcher maths' in primary schools: the material would be prepared directly for the pupils, involving the teacher only as organiser and presenter;

(4) the material would have to fit like a puzzle-piece into the existing classroom situation, without making additional demands on the teacher and without disturbing normal school and classroom routine.

Finding the expertise

Of all the parts of the curriculum innovation system, the most difficult to achieve is the supply of systems/programming skills. This is largely a resource problem, as an experienced analyst/programmer currently 'sells' for over £200 per day, yet the classroom materials were known to take about 100 man-hours per class hour to produce. At £20,000 per class hour, the situation is clearly impossible; cheaper inexperienced people such as teachers had not produced reliable materials that could be used in the classroom. A supply of trained people became available through the UMIST B.Sc. Computation degree programme, whereby each third year student had to complete a 200-hour computing project in order to fulfill the requirements for the degree.

When a lasting change occurs in a system, it is usually when the change constitutes a solution to a real problem. In this case, the UMIST students and the teachers both had real problems, and between them a bridge was built to provide the 'missing link' between computing subject/technology and the classroom teaching material. The computer applications in their 'raw' state in commerce and industry were usually large and difficult to understand, poorly documented and explained, and in many cases extremely complex technologically. Because the teachers could not cope with the technology, each student went to a computer application site on his own and prepared a full set of documentation of an application system. This documentation formed the basis on which the teachers then prepared a pupil text about the application and a set of class exercises.

Keeping within the limits

At each stage of the curriculum development process, the known constraints to the classroom teaching situation were applied. For example,

- the need to cover other areas of the examination syllabus limited the study of applications to no more than four weeks, unless other computing topics could be brought into the material;
- having only one microcomputer per class, the three-minute limit was imposed on the materials to be prepared for the computer;
- similarly, a maximum of 45 keystrokes was imposed on each pupil's computer exercise;
- the need to keep order in the classroom required other related materials to be prepared for 'seat work' — the calculations showed that these materials would need to take up four times as much time as the computer exercises;
- slow reading speeds and vocabulary weaknesses in mixed-ability classes required careful use and clarification of words used in text and exercises;
- likewise, care in design of computer dialogue was necessary — no presumptions could be made that words on the screen would actually be read and understood;

- materials prepared would have to be capable of mass production so that the cost for four lessons (one week's work) would not exceed 10p per pupil;
- the computer programs would have to be run by the pupils themselves without the teacher's assistance, and they would have to be 'idiot-proof' and 'vandal-proof';
- material and exercises of differing levels of difficulty were needed to provide for the broad range of abilities in the mixed-ability class.

Putting it together

During the stage in which the actual teaching materials were produced, the UMIST students worked closely with the teachers, coordinating what was possible on the computer with what was needed for the classroom. This was a back-and-forth juggling and development process, and it was also a learning process for both students and teachers.

While designing the three-minute pupil interaction with the computer, the UMIST students made extensive reference to material on system design – in particular, on-line system design and microcomputer file and program design – and they drew on material from other parts of their Computation course, especially programming methods. Commodore contributed their internal programming standards, and Cytek (UK) Ltd's screen- and file-handling techniques were adapted by the students to make the programs run faster and more reliably.

This process drew into the materials the absent elements from the computer subject/technology system which are normally not directly involved in curriculum development.

The computer programs were subjected to rigorous testing before they were used in the classroom. Error conditions and slow timing (when first tried, all four programs took over 15 minutes to run) were dealt with mainly by programming refinements until the programs could be run despite a wide variety of wrong inputs within three minutes and 45 keystrokes. Some of the computer exercise material was also changed to achieve a better 'fit'.

The project group gave a great deal of attention to how the materials would be used in the classroom as a system. In particular, they tried to follow the normal classroom teaching pattern and sequence: lead lesson and demonstration by the teacher, doing identical exercises, then doing other related exercises. To ensure enforcement of learning with regard to the computer exercises, the group agreed on establishing groups of pupils who would spend at least 15 minutes at the computer. They also felt that if one child used the computer on his own and could not cope, he could lose out, whereas as part of a group other children would be able to provide help and advice to the less able, and by watching other children using the computer on similar but not identical material, he would gain a richer picture of the application under study.

Timing of group schedules, numbers of pupils in groups, and numbers of groups of pupils were assessed for their 'fit' within the classroom situation.

Calculation of group change-over times and set-up times presuming the 'worst' case in which computer studies was taught in four different and separate time-table slots led to the conclusion that there should be at least four and not more then six groups; there should be at least three and not more than six pupils in each group. In addition, a teaching schedule emerged:

(1) lead lesson and demonstration: first lesson, no more than 30 minutes;
(2) computer exercise, each group 15 minutes;
(3) 'seat work' exercises, designed to take up 80% of class work time, to be completed by pupils before and after the computer exercises.

Neither the computer exercise nor the 'seat work' exercises could be dependent on one another, because pupils would be doing them at different times. Both exercises, however, could be dependent upon the lead lesson and demonstration and upon the pupil text.

Evaluating the materials in use in the classroom

When the materials were tried out in the classroom, the UMIST students removed themselves from active participation in their development and use. They became evaluators of the system as it functioned in the classroom; in particular, they measured the following:

• legibility of words and other material on the TV screen during the teacher's demonstration lesson;
• where pupils were sitting in the classroom, and whether they continued to look at the screen and the teacher, or to look away;
• any time lag during which the teacher had to wait for computer response, and any inappropriate responses by the compter program;
• length of time each pupil and each group took to do the computer exercises, and any errors that occured during the computer runs;
• number of times the teacher had to clarify or intervene to enable the pupils to carry on with the computer exercise;
• whether the 'seat work' exercises were enough to keep all members of the class busy for the entire week;
• amount of preparation and set-up time by the teacher for the first lesson, and for the week's work.

For people involved in more traditional methods of curriculum evaluation, these factors might seem inappropriate.[11] The project was based on systems methods throughout, and evaluation was carried out on the classroom performance of a designed system. Use of these methods was adopted because traditional curriculum evaluation techniques do not deal with the logistics of classroom use of materials with sufficient precision to establish whether they are within feasible limits of performance.

One of the four sets of computer studies materials required substantial adjustment at this stage, but the other three sets performed within the original design specifications.

Delivering the materials

Developing a set of curriculum materials is one task; actually delivering materials into the classroom so that they are used is quite another. For this part of the process, Addison-Wesley Ltd were involved to put the materials in their final form. To keep the cost per pupil per lesson low, a simple plastic-wrapped pack was decided upon, in which a diskette or tape would be inserted along with spirit masters containing the pupil text and exercise pages. A teacher's manual is also included in the pack. The price range of each pack is £15–18; considering that the pack should last for about five years and reach a minimum of 40 pupils a year, the cost per pupil for a week's lessons would be around the 10p limit.

Normal commercial channels for the distribution of educational materials were considered essential to the long-term impact of the materials.

1.6 PROSPECTS FOR CURRICULUM DEVELOPMENT

The lessons learned in the computer studies project have been applied to a commercial order-processing system to identify and cure where possible the causes of data processing errors and problems occuring in a newly-installed part of the system. They have helped to firm up some ideas about the structure and necessary functions of systems in general, to enable analysts to spot missing or weak system functions.[12]

But the lessons about curriculum development are going to be a lot harder to get across. It is so easy to fudge results in a curriculum development project, and so difficult to obtain reliable figures. The school system in general tends to incorporate even the most unsuitable changes over the short term; but it tends to restore equilibrium in the long term, carrying on much as before according to the logistic priorities by which it survives. If we can learn to establish specific working limits for classroom materials, and to prepare materials to fit within those limits, there is much valuable work to be done. If we cannot, we owe the tax- and rate-payers who pay our salaries our best efforts in some other endeavour that is more likely to bear fruit. And we owe it to school pupils to devote our skills and energies to filling their minds and fitting their fingers with activities more likely to enable them to survive in the adult world.

The Manchester project goes on; next year a further four application sets will be prepared, to meet the same criteria. Meanwhile, the curriculum innovation system's effectiveness will not be known for at least five years; this effectiveness will be judged by only one criterion: whether the materials are still used in the secondary school classroom, having become incorporated into the fabric of the system, or whether they will have joined the ranks of the bright ideas that do not work in the classroom.

REFERENCES

[1] Wiseman, S. and Pidgeon, D. *Curriculum Evaluation*, National Foundation for Educational Research in England and Wales, 1972.

[2] Eraut, M. 'The Impact of Educational Technology on Curriculum Development', *Curriculum Innovation in Practice*, Edge Hill College of Education, 1969.

[3] Halsey, P. 'Curriculum Innovation: National efforts', *ibid.*

[4] Gross, N., Giacquinta, J. and Bernstein, M., *Implementing Organizational Innovations*, Harper & Row, 1971.

[5] Glans, *et al. Management Systems*, Holt Rinehart, 1968.

[6] Bell, R., *et al.* 'The question of curriculum change in the context of GCE examination boards', *Education in Great Britain and Ireland*, Routledge & Kegan Paul, 1973.

[7] Eyferth, K., *et al. Computer-unterstützter Unterricht in der allgemeinbildenden Schule*, Bildungs-technologisches Zentrum Weisbaden, 1973.

[8] Bayliss, S., 'Pupil-teacher ratio worsening', *Times Education Supplement*, 25.9.81, p. 12.

[9] Reid, W. and Walker, D., *Case Studies in Curriculum Change*, Routledge & Kegan Paul, 1975.

[10] Miller, J., *Living Systems*, McGraw-Hill, 1978.

[11] Shipman, M., *et al. Inside a Curriculum Project*, Methuen, 1974.

[12] Hennessey, A. and Ahmad, F., 'Error-based analysis of information system interfacing', UMIST Department of Computation, 1981.

CHAPTER 2

Mechanism for CAL origination

Bob Lewis, St. Martin's College, Lancaster

Bob Lewis was formerly Reader in Computer Assisted Education, Chelsea College, University of London, and Director, Schools Council Project, 'Computers in the Curriculum'. Part of this paper is based on a paper presented to the Italian Computer Society in September 1981.

2.1 CURRICULAE RESOURCES REQUIRED FOR CAL

Before examining the mechanism for the development of CAL material it is necessary to place CAL (as the acronym will be used) in perspective.

The most valuable, and at one time the only, educational resource is the human teacher. Originally, at an academic level these teachers were philosophers and at a practical level were parents. Over the centuries, technology has provided learners with more resources, books, films, scientific apparatus and so on. With the addition of each resource the domain of what could be learnt expanded. Within the framework of institutional learning teachers became providers of learning resources rather than the only resource. Curriculae are devised to reflect the needs or fundamentals of each discipline and each new resource influences curriculae in the sense that its design is a function of what *can* be learnt.

As a physicist the most obvious new resource available to me when I was a teacher was certain apparatus for the laboratory. New apparatus (from Leybold, Teltron, etc.) made it possible to involve students in learning about atomic and nuclear physics in ways hitherto impossible. As an individual teacher, I changed the emphasis in my courses and soon the curriculum was redefined to reflect such changes by many physics teachers. If it can be demonstrated that the computer is a valuable learning resource, then in time the curriculum will reflect this.

It is now logical to examine possible roles for the computer as a learning resource, to see what learning opportunities it may offer and to assess its value. It will have been noticed perhaps that in discussing resources I have spoken entirely about *learning*. Now there is a Chinese proverb which is often quoted but which I do not hesitate to quote again because it reflects most clearly the nearest I ever get to a learning theory in the formal sense:

> I hear, I forget
> I see, I remember
> I do, I understand.

So 'doing', that is some activity, is important if we wish learners to understand. A teacher-centred approach is based on a behaviour view of learning as described by Skinner and Gagne. In contrast the approach favoured in our work with computers has been learner centred. An extract in a Research Report from the Department of Artificial Intelligence in Edinburgh describes the flavour of our attitude succinctly.

1   Learning is gathering information which is represented in complex mental structures. Collectively, these structures constitute our knowledge of the world. Besides storing information about physical objects, the mental structures represent a hierarchy of concepts and relationships which are derived from accumulated information by the operation of generalisation and differentiation processes.

2   Gathering information comes about through activity. This includes actions in the physical environment (for example, play) through which information about objects, events and people is gathered directly; and internal (mental operations) in the environment as represented symbolically through speech, writing systems, number systems, by means of which information is gathered indirectly. Until the child can use these symbolic methods of getting information, his information gathering activities will bring him into direct contact with reality.

3   Motivation is a pre-requisite of activity. Suppose we assume that the child has an in-built drive to explore. Through actions in the environment, information about particular objects, particular events and particular people becomes embedded in mental structures. As these structures develop, their very existence will begin to shape the learner's actions, introducing the kind of consistent behaviour associated with a well-motivated child. Conversely, impeding spontaneous activity will inhibit the growth of mental structure, and the child's level of motivation will diminish.

4   Information gathering should be organized. As Piaget points out, a child will build idiosyncratic explanations of real phenomena on the basis of restricted knowledge. It is important to realise that these explanations are not wrong (usually); they are invalid in the context of our model of physical reality but not in terms of the child's impoverished model. This implies that complex learning cannot be regulated solely by the

child's own interest, but must be carefully organised so that the information content of the mental structure can be altered to bring it into closer correspondence with reality [1].

The computer's role in this is as an information resource. In particular, its function is not to assess the student's performance and control any future information provided. This was the main role in most of the early work on computerised teaching machines in the 1960s and there are concerns about this of which I have written elsewhere [2]. The computer (plus its software of course) should provide information for the learner in the way that apparatus in a laboratory does. In order to provide some structure to the student's gathering of information (required by Howe in point 4 above) we select a sequence of problems for the student to investigate. These problems are chosen by experienced teachers in such a way as to help the student in his exploration of a certain field.

The components of our Computer Assisted Learning (CAL) materials are thus:

(a) Student problem sheets/leaflets
(b) An interactive computer program
(c) A guide for the teacher

The following is an extract from a Students' Leaflet for the unit on Pond Ecology in the Computers in the Biology Curriculum pack.

B1   What happens to the numbers of herbivores when the initial fish number is altered? If fish are entirely absent, does the number of herbivores increase indefinitely?

B2   What is the effect of changing the initial number of herbivores on the numbers of (a) fish, and (b) phytoplankton?

B3   How does the number of phytoplankton affect the herbivore and fish numbers?

B4   You will have found that the numbers of organisms are not constant throughout the year. What do you think causes the number of phytoplankton to increase and decrease? Suggest why the number of herbivores gets larger and smaller throughout the year.

B5   Suggest the thing or things that control the numbers of (a) phytoplankton, (b) herbivores and (c) fish.

B6   Compare the numbers of phytoplankton, herbivores and fish in the pond. Why do you think the numbers decrease as you pass from phytoplankton to herbivores to fish?

The interactive program associated with this topic is a simulation of an ecological system. The program contains a model of the system to be simulated and a natural language interaction takes place between student and program.

The interaction may take a number of forms; what we term a dialogue form is illustrated here in a program supporting a study of the chemical principles involved in the commercial manufacture of sulphuric acid.

WHAT IS TEMPERATURE   (DEG C) ? 700
WHAT IS THE INITIAL MOLAR RATIO SO2:O2
(TYPE TWO NUMBERS SEPARATED BY A COMMA)
? 5,3
WHAT IS PRESSURE (ATM) ? 5
DO YOU WANT TO USE THE CATALYST? NO

MAXIMUM POSSIBLE CONVERSION
    OF SO2 IS   59%

USING ONE CONVERTER 25.3 TONNES
OF SULPHURIC ACID IS PRODUCED PER DAY.

Finally, a guide is required for the teacher who is to use the material. Many teachers are unfamiliar with the use of CAL materials and so are grateful for advice from their author-colleagues. In a unit on Windmill Location, chosen as a simple example of the general principles of Industrial Location, in the Computers in the Geography Curriculum pack, the Teachers' Guide suggests a sequence of work based on the Students' Leaflets:

The students' material is designed for flexibility so that the simulation can fit into many different teaching contexts. The central core of the simulation is in Leaflets C and D. Leaflet E is likely to be a relevant immediate follow-up to the students' work on the computer terminal. The rest of the student material is optional and different approaches could be used without affecting the success of the simulation itself.

The teacher may not wish to spend any class time on an historical or technical study of windmills, so the first part of the introductory work that prepares students for the simulation is optional. This contained in Students' Leaflet A, which covers how grain is turned into flour and the accompanying diagram of a windmill mechanism on Leaflet B. If it is desired to cover this topic, these leaflets could be used as a worksheet, following class discussion on how different parts of the mill might work. Samples of what is produced at different stages in the milling process are available (see Section 5.6, references and teaching materials), and could be studied by the students at this stage.

2.2 CAL AS A CURRICULUM RESOURCE

It is perhaps worth stressing now that the designers and authors of CAL materials should be first and foremost experienced teachers of the discipline, say, biology or geography. CAL materials are developed to add to the resources in the coverage of various curriculae. It is the teachers of those curriculae who know what kind of resource is likely to prove its value to students in that field.

An evolution in approach has taken place and is appropriate here. The early applications for CAL in our science work can be viewed as extensions of problem solving associated with laboratory investigations. The work then extended to role playing and decision making simulations and games in geography and economics. The sciences and geography areas also included CAL material associated with field studies and industrial applications. Whilst all the work was based on models of the relevant systems, these were largely defined for the learner and our attempts at setting problems in which the learner had to construct his own models were not successful. Some material illustrated alternative models but, without demanding a fairly high degree of programming ability, we were not able to encourage the true exploration of theoretical ideas. In connection with physics education we are concerned with just this kind of exploration [3]. In the professional world simulation languages do exist but these are designed for other purposes and require a degree of commitment not appropriate for the majority of students. A simple model building language was required [4] more commensurate with the goals of student problem solving. In order to provide the tools to enable students to undertake what we term 'experimental mathematics', Hartley [5] devised a suitable language system on a microcomputer. Our use of this language is experimental at the moment but we believe that it is capable of providing the right kind of experience for non-computer specialists in order that model building, the exploration of theoretical ideas, can be introduced more fruitfully into secondary and tertiary level courses.

A final but crucial point relates to the impact which CAL could have on the curriculum itself. In our work during the 1970s, we selected topics for a CAL treatment which were already a part of the existing curriculum. This was necessary as, amongst other reasons, we had to develop a methodology which would be acceptable to present-day teachers. The result is that the topics covered are rather randomly spread across the various curriculae. There is no uniform pattern and we had to justify the use of CAL as providing a new unique resource.

However, as we move into the 1980s we are now emphasising the influence CAL can have on

(a) the curriculum content, and

(b) the whole style of learning.

The potential influence on the mathematics curriculum has been recently described in the MIT Press Series in Artificial Intelligence, [6]. Our new work in science, geography, history and economics is all linked with new UK curriculum development projects in those areas which exist for reasons quite unconnected with microcomputer availability in schools. We hope that our experience in CAL development can complement those projects' understanding of the need for curriculum change.

2.3 DEVELOPMENT ALTERNATIVES IN CAL PRODUCTION

A detailed account of the structure and methodology of the Chelsea Projects is given in a recent review paper [7]. However, it is necessary for me to give an outline of this here. The computers in the Curriculum Project supported by the Schools Council and, now in addition, by the DES Microelectronics Education Project is the basis of this outline.

The need to involve practising teachers in the development of materials has already been stressed. Consequently, it was natural that the Project should be decentralised. In close collaboration with LEA advisers, groups of teachers with a particular curriculum experience were formed in various parts of the country. Centrally, we tried to support these groups with services, secretarial, technical etc., and coordinated the development through a series of national panels. A trials organisation was also established to provide peer-review of the draft materials. In view of its national responsibility the Project had to ensure that the materials produced were educationally acceptable and technically portable. In other words they had to be acceptable as resources to teachers and had to be capable of direct implementation on whatever computer hardware was available. It was necessary for us to be able to create materials concerning which a teacher would answer in the affirmative the two questions:

> Do I *want* to use the materials?
> *Can* I use (run) the program?

A considerable effort is needed to achieve these goals, effort in terms of manpower and facilities. It is also essential to provide an aftercare service as is available following the purchase of any technical materials or equipment. The consequence of such a policy is that the materials take time to produce, and to put into publishable form with the necessary back-up. And the development costs are considerable. These drawbacks can only be justified if the eventual take-up of the material is large and this requires a major dissemination exercise. To aid the latter we required the professional services of an educational publisher and, of course, the decentralised nature of the Project assisted this dissemination process.

The aims and problems associated with a large scale project have been outlined. The most common other source of material is that produced by individual teachers and sometimes this is contributed to a 'user group' or other collection. In one sense this costs nothing to produce and may be quite cheap to buy. Some of it is well produced with full supporting material and is in all ways excellent as an educational resource. However, much of it has serious defects:

- the software may only be available as a listing;
- the software may not be technically documented;
- the software may be implemented in only one particular environment;
- the educational aims may be dubious or at least poorly described;
- the courseware, even some teachers' notes, may be scant or non-existant;
- technical and educational back-up may be completely absent.

For an experienced microcomputer teacher/user, one or more of these defects may be easily overcome. However, there is a hidden cost in overcoming such problems as there is in the origination itself. Much more seriously, the newcomer to the resource is unable to compensate for the inadequacies and is prejudiced in his views about the potential the resource offers.

To overcome the problems described it is important to set acceptance criteria for materials which are contributed to CAL 'libraries'. These need to be formally defined and strictly enforced. It is not clear that a range of standards from 'first class' to 'use it at your peril' is workable. The fine distinction between categories is difficult to draw and will in any case be a function of the end-user's experience.

The distribution agency with which I have had close contact is CONDUIT†. Their materials are not cheap in the UK but their vetting procedures and hence the quality of their materials is good. This remark is not intended as a criticism of UK organisations working on less formal lines. However, it would be of benefit to the educational community at large if we all looked critically at our current practices. A few years ago an article in CONDUIT's journal *PIPELINE* discussed the effort required in developing computer assisted materials. The point was well made that originating a 'package' for use by one's own students and finding it successful was only a fifth of the way down the road to making it useful for others. Not many originators are prepared to expend the extra effort required in completing the process.

2.4 TECHNICAL CONSIDERATIONS FOR CAL DISSEMINATION

A few words may not be amiss at this point in order to give some idea of the technical directions in which Computers in the Curriculum has been progressing. As has been said before the creation of educational material is labour intensive.

The resources involved in this creation demand that the material created is widely disseminated and acceptable. This means that the software element must be transferable between hardware systems. Most educational material has been developed using the language BASIC as this language was the most common interactive language of the 1970s. Equally it is the most commonly used language on microcomputers. Used with some care, this language, in a minimal sub-set form, proved to be adequate for CAL development during the last decade. However, the facilities of present day microcomputers and the anticipated facilities of the future, mean that an approach to transferability via syntactic standards is no longer adequate. These considerations have led us to shift from syntactic standards on which we had depended (compatible with ANSI minimal BASIC), to functional standards. The saving grace is that there are a finite

†CONDUIT, P.O. Box 388, Iowa City, Iowa 42244.

number of microcomputer systems. We have thus found it possible to adopt the functional standards approach by defining a hypothetical system and producing software for a variety of hardware/firmware environments which emulate this hypothetical system. From an applications viewpoint this means that we develop CAL software for the hypothetical system and can do this using ANSI minimal BASIC. In order to achieve the hypothetical system we have written a *Software Library* [8] for each hardware/firmware system which creates a common environment. This was based, in philosophy, on a Graphics Library developed for mainframe driven graphics terminals used in an earlier project [9]. Much of the Library is the same for all systems as it has a hierarchical structure and only a few primitive routines need to be system dependent. The remainder of the Library provides a set of graphical and other display utility routines to aid software writing. Due to the structure of the library it offers another important facility. In an age when the technology is changing so rapidly, new devices (for input and output) are becoming available to microcomputer users all the time. The modular structure of the Library allows us to add 'driver-routines' for such new devices and, with only a parameter value change in a program, these can be used by existing CAL programs. In this way we hope to protect ourselves from the danger of writing software for a technology which soon finds itself out-of-date. The evolution of our material to make use of speech hardware, video-disks, graphical tablets, full colour displays, should be possible without major disturbance to our overall software structure.

Another important software consideration concerns flexibility in defining the form of the learner-software interface. Most of our early material was written with a fixed dialogue form. This was easy to use by the learner but could be a little tedious to use once the learner became fully familiar with the program. It also made it difficult for the teacher to adapt a program to a form more suitable for a particular group of students. Some of our programs which had many parameters were written to allow single parameter changes.

We have now changed to a completely *keyword* driven form of interaction but we have been able to retain the dialogue form none-the-less. Each basic function of our programs is initiated by the user through the choice of a specific keyword. In addition to these primitive keywords, we are able to link together a sequence of keywords by defining secondary keywords. The method of defining these is by simply adding DATA statements to the program. This means that a teacher who is not a programmer can adapt the interaction to his/her own particular needs. By linking a variable to a keyword it is also possible to create an interaction in which parameters of the model take on default values and so the model may be made as complex or simple for the student as is *educationally desirable*. Whilst the keyword structure for programs is primarily aimed at increasing the flexibility offered to teacher-users of our CAL material, we hope that it will prove to aid the definition of required software by teacher-authors. The possibility exists that a complete program specification can be provided for a programmer using the Library and the keyword protocols by the following definitions:

- primary keywords to be used and their function including error or warning conditions;
- a definition of the model or a structure for the decision rules;
- sample sketches of screen displays at various output stages.

A paper for authors/developers on the use of the Library and keywords is available from the Project [10].

2.5 THE FUTURE

The Computers in the Curriculum Project has lived through most dramatic advances in technology and attitude towards computers in education. We entered the 1970s with some tentative educational ideas and now see a technology sufficiently developed for our educational rationale to become a reality. Without doubt the next decade will see the availability of the technology in all our formal institutes of learning for children of five years old onwards and in addition the use of computer assisted learning in the home and in many other informal ways. We still don't use broadcast television to its greatest potential in our homes and it is likely that any delay in making use of computer resources will not be due to the lack or cheapness of the technology but to our lack of imagination and the resources to create adequate learning opportunities. However quickly the technology develops, the real benefits will only accrue if we concern ourselves with its educational value.

Acknowledgements

Our original work was supported by the Shell grant to Chelsea College for Mathematics Education. The Schools Council for the Curriculum and Examinations has provided backing since 1972 and the Department of Education and Science through its Microelectronics Education Programme since 1980. Throughout all the work Chelsea College has provided the basic facilities.

The extracts of CAL material used in this paper were taken from the Computers in the Curriculum Project materials (Phase I) published by the Schools Council.

REFERENCES

[1] J. A. M. Howe., A. Beattie., F. Cassels., J. Johnson, and A. Anderson, *Teaching Handicapped Children to Read in a Computer-Based Learning Environment, D. A. I. Research Report No. 57,* Edinburgh, 1978.

[2] R. Lewis, Pedagogical Issues in Designing Programs in (Eds. Howe and Ross) *Microcomputers in Secondary Education,* London, Kogan Page, 1981.

[3] R. Lewis and J. Harris, 'Physics Education With or Without Computers,' *Computers and Education*, 4, 1, 1980.

[4] R. D. Harding, 'Towards a new computer language', in Lewis, (Ed.) *Computers in the Life Sciences*, Croom Helm, 1979.

[5] R. J. Hartley, *MODL – An Interactive Computer System for Mathematical Modelling by Non-specialists*, PhD thesis, Chelsea College, London, 1981.

[6] H. Abelsom, and A. di Sessa, *Turtle Geometry*, MIT Press, 1981.

[7] R. Lewis and D. Want, 'Educational Computing at Chelsea (1969-79)', in Lewis and Tagg, (Eds.) *Computer Assisted Learning*, North Holland, Amsterdam, 1980 and Heinemann, London 1981.

[8] P. W. Smith, *et al. A CAL Software Library Manual*, London, Schools Council/Chelsea College, 1981.

[9] J. Mckenzie, L. R. B., Elton, and R. Lewis, (Eds.), *Interactive Computer Graphics in Science Teaching*, Ellis Horwood, 1978.

[10] R. Lewis, and D. Want (Eds.) *Project Paper 20 CAL materials – design, guidelines and standards*, London, Schools Council/Chelsea College, 1981.

CHAPTER 3

In-service micro courses for the teaching profession

David Burghes, School of Education, Exeter University

3.1 THE MICRO AS AN EDUCATIONAL RESOURCE

All those concerned with the educational use of micros are, I am sure, delighted to see the number of machines in schools and colleges rising rapidly. This is despite yet more cuts in educational budgets. It is a measure of the enthusiasm of some staff and LEA advisers (and pupils and parents) that it will not be long before it will be quite difficult to find a secondary school without at least one machine, whilst those schools who bought their first machine a year or more ago will probably now have several machines and will be planning for a computer laboratory in the not too distant future. This is the optimistic side.

On the pessimistic side is the fact that the vast majority of time spent by pupils and staff on these machines is concerned with the teaching of computer studies (particularly at CSE but also now significantly at 'O' and 'A' level). Although I realise that there are exceptions to this rule, I am sure that they are the exceptions, and that overall I would estimate that at least 90% of usage is directed to computer studies teaching. Of course, it is not difficult to see why this is happening; the major justification that state schools can give for buying micros is that they are teaching computer studies (or planning to do so) and it would be highly convenient for the school to have its own computing power — which is both cheap, relatively trouble free, and fully under the schools control — in comparison to either using telephone links, postal service to the local poly. or town hall computer, or, as happens in many cases, taking the pupils to terminals at the local technical college or poly. Having justified the purchase of the micro in order to help in the teaching of computer studies, it must of course be used for this purpose — and this is when the real difficulties start; for, with an eye clearly on job prospects, computer studies, particularly at CSE, have become a very popular subject to opt for. Table 3.1 shows the figures for examination entries in computer studies for the past few years.

Table 3.1

Year	CSE	GCE 'O' Level	GCE 'AO' Level	GCE 'A' Level	CSE	Total
1975	8785	1335	–	1340	–	11460
1976	13181	3217	116	1512	–	18026
1977	15218	6091	109	1764	–	23182
1978	15489	8417	511	1769	233	26419
1979	16210	11635	765	2323	591	31524
1980	18001	14907	1049	2819	635	37411

The total figures show an astonishing increase with the figures still rapidly increasing. This means that in our 'typical' comprehensive, our micro, say, is being used by 90 or more pupils who are taking a CSE in computer studies. It is not surprising that, even in the most well managed school, very few people outside those involved in computer studies will ever get much of a chance to even see a micro, let alone get to use it. This situation contrasts with the many and varied potential uses that microcomputers have in education; for example:

- Computer assisted learning (CAL)
- Computer manager learning
- Simulations in biology, geography, physics, economics, history, etc.,
- Control in experiments
- Word processing
- School administration

Of course a second important reason for the use of micros in teaching computer studies rather than for the uses above is that as yet we just do not have software of the right quality and robustness to support these applications. The potential of the microcomputer as an EDUCATIONAL RESOURCE right across the curriculum is vast, but there are many many major hurdles to be overcome, if we are really to fully exploit this potential.

3.2 TEACHER RESISTANCE TO A NEW RESOURCE

Although, at the present time, there is clearly an enormous amount of enthusiasm for micros in education, I think it should be realised that this enthusiasm is *not* shared by all the teaching profession. Some regard the advent of the micro as just another new toy, and that the enthusiasm from boffins in the mathematics department will soon decline. Others take a very defensive role simply because they are scared. Firstly, 'scared' because of lack of information – they do not really know what the microcomputer is and what it can do, and they don't want to show their ignorance either to their superiors (who might well be equally worried) or to their juniors (who might well know all about it). Secondly, they are scared because of the fear that CAL will make the teacher's role redundant and that in the future, pupils will be going to the computer school for all their tuition! If we are really going to exploit the full educational potential, we ignore these fears and worries at our peril.

Once we have mastered the micro, the computer expert soon becomes immersed in the technical jargon of the computer – 'printout', 'floppies', 'cursor', 'RAM', 'ROM' – whilst the novice is still trying to grasp the difference between hardware and software. I think it is very difficult for us to understand how the novice feels faced with a boffin who is talking a different language and a machine which he is frightened to touch. Now I know this is not true of many teachers, but I suspect it is true for the majority – the teachers who up to now have not got involved with the micro. If we are going to really use the micro across the curriculum, it is these teachers who need the right sort of in-service training. It is easy enough to find in a school a couple of teachers willing and able to become computer experts – it is going to be much more difficult to convince the rest of the staff that the micro can become an invaluable educational resource which they will actually use.

It must be appreciated that most adults have this in-built inhibition to a new technology, and teachers are a representative set of adults, and it is no disgrace that many have this fear. As the experts, we must first realise this fact and learn how to handle it. It is of interest to note that these adult inhibitions are not present in most children. They are quite willing to learn by trial and error, as they do in most other areas. Their minds are open to a new technology – it is part of their life – after all the computer age has been with them for some time through television programmes such as *Dr. Who, Blake's Seven* and *Startrek*.

3.3 IN-SERVICE COURSES

As I mentioned before there are still many hurdles to be overcome if we are really to make the whole teaching profession aware of the micro's potential (as well as its limitations). If, for example, CAL work is to really take off in education (and I believe that it will eventually) then we clearly need more and more keyboards and VDU's (Visual Display Units) in the classroom – and, more than that, we need the sound educational and robust software. But even if these problems are solved, we will still need a massive in-service package if we are to get teachers to use the resources (and not just for teachers, but also for advisers, heads and administrators).

Courses at various levels will be needed. Let me first deal with the introductory level – in many ways I think that this is the most difficult to solve. In order to utilise this new resource (when it is fully available) we need to have all the teaching profession fully proficient at operating the available hardware, as well as being aware of what capabilities and limitations the resource has. I have outlined below a typical three-day introductory course for micros, which has these aims.

Day 1 Introduction

Session 1 — Introduction to Microprocessors and Microcomputing (General information — hardware and software — some introductory simulations and CAL software).

Session 2 — Participants use pre-written tapes/discs; with, if possible, as many micros as participants.

Session 3 — Discussion of what has been achieved so far, and an introduction to cursor control, listing and very elementary programming.

Session 4 — Individual work with micros — familiarisation of keyboard, cursor control, typing short programmes, listing and editing.

Day 2 Programming

This whole day is devoted to participants writing elementary programmes; firstly for suggested tasks, and secondly for tasks suggested by each participant. The day must be interspersed with elementary programming tuition, although the main aim should be for each participant to have their own programme working by the end of the day rather than have a comprehensive programming tuition.

Day 3 Educational Resource

Session 1 — Introduction to the use of the micro in CAL work.

Session 2 — Introduction to the use of the micro in simulation and control.

Session 3 — Final practical session.

Session 4 — Discussion of the micro as an educational resource.

Having taught introductory micro courses for two years now, although I am still not clear how much programming knowledge the 'average' teacher needs, I am convinced that some elementary programming knowledge is needed, and that knowledge is best obtained in a practical rather than systematic manner. For example, if a participant wants to sort a list of names into alphabetical order, then the motivation for learning to cope with loops is immediately there. I am also convinced that the ideal situation is one participant to one micro — initially I felt the optimum number would be two per micro, and while this might be true for children, I am now certain that for adults, a machine for each participant is the ideal situation.

What is also needed is firm but sympathetic handling. With each participant having a micro in front of them, they are forced to actually use it — this is quite crucial, as if several people are round one micro, it is very easy for someone to opt out, pretend to be following all that is going on, but never actually get their hands on the machine. So participants must be forced to get involved rather then take a back seat, but also a very sympathetic attitude on the part of the trainer is needed. Remember that a complete novice really doesn't know what to do, doesn't know what keys to push and doesn't like to admit it! I think it is always a good idea to have some instructions for operation printed out — although help from the tutor will probably still be needed.

One point worth noting here is that the PET is an excellent micro for introductory courses — I particularly still like the integral 8K machine for use with complete newcomers. It just requires plugging in, switching on and then it is ready — not only that, there are no nasty wires to connect anywhere and it is fully portable. I do sincerely hope that in the development of the next generation of machines, this integral concept will not be lost altogether.

So much for introductory courses; this is of course only the start, but for many teachers it will be sufficient for their needs. When the specialist subject software is available, they will have the confidence to use it and to contemplate modifying it. They will also have learnt the language, and will not be frightened to talk about the use of the micro in their subject area. The next level of courses are far more optional in nature — word processing, administration, timetabling, control, interfacing data processing, and basic software writing. These are all areas of great need, but unless one can put on successful introductory courses, there will be fewer takers for the next level.

One way in which to encourage further training in the micro area would be the initiation of part-time M.Sc. or M.Ed. courses in 'Educational Computing'. In this way, not only would teachers (who are of course now moving towards an all-graduate profession) be learning about the new technology and its educational potential, but would be adding a further qualification. I suspect that many teachers would be willing to finance themselves for such a course, as it would clearly not only increase their ability to develop and use the new technology but would also enhance their promotion prospects.

3.4 THE FUTURE EXPLOITATION

I have deliberately avoided discussing some of the other major hurdles in exploiting micros to the full as an educational potential — partly, because I really don't have any real answers, but equally because I take the optimistic view that these problems will get sorted out in time. I am certainly convinced that computing power will get cheaper, that more keyboards will be available for use, and, crucially, the excellent software so urgently needed will get written. In this connection, I feel that commercial publishers must be increasingly involved, and that we shouldn't regard this as a retrograde step. Many individuals developing software for their own and local use are to be encouraged, but at some stage there must be a systematic approach to the development of professional educational software.

So I am optimistic on these points — but I am not so optimistic that the teaching profession will in fact fully utilise this exciting resource. While we clearly have a large number of experts now, are we really successfully educating the whole profession? I have serious doubts, and if we fail to do so successfully, I can imagine a situation when we have a little-used educational resource — micros gathering dust in cupboards! It is already apparent that many pupils in schools are far ahead in their computer knowledge and expertise. Many teachers will find this a threat so it is up to us, as the initial experts, to become the sympathetic trainers of the rest of the profession. We must make sure that we are outward looking rather than giving the impression of an introverted closed circle of computer boffins.

CHAPTER 4

The role of the Local Education Authorities

Keith Tomlinson, Bradford Metropolitan Council

4.1 IS THERE A ROLE FOR THE LEA TO PLAY?

Yes! However, it can be negative, neutral or positive. My own belief is that the LEA should play a *positive* central co-ordinating, enabling role. However, lets first look at the other possibilities.

Negative

The negative LEA will adopt the 'Luddite' approach, banning the use of micros in schools, and taking the stance that this is another innovation which the already overburdened Education Budget cannot stand. This stance may apparently work for a short time but many ingenious teachers will quietly circumvent it buying micros but calling them laboratory equipment, mathematical calculators, A/V aids and even in some cases using their own equipment — unfortunately having to be sercretive will deny these adventurous, inventive enthusiasts access to joint work and encourage them to move on to greener pastures. But it will not stop the introduction of microcomputers. This stance is now, of course, becoming less tenable because of the government's initiative.

Neutral

A neutral stance is often associated with large bodies: the ponderous decision-making process and the innumerable committees make it more comfortable to sit back and watch rather than do.

Many authorities will prefer this, bemoaning the lack of staff, resources, cut-backs etc. Or questioning whether the 'time is right' or not, or the significance of changing the educational curriculum, and whether or not computers will contribute to producing a 'rounded' individual; in fact very much the same arguments as the negatives but laden with educational jargon about the individual learning process etc., totally ignoring the fact that in the real world computers are here to stay!

Everyone on leaving school will be involved with computers — at work; clock cards, banks, supermarket tills, at leisure; computer games, computerised booking for recreation and entertainment and even in unemployment (benefits, rents, rebates). All these items depend on computers and it will leave today's generation ill-equipped for the modern world if school has not given them an insight into the uses and misuses of computers.

Again computers will invade schools in these neutral areas via active parents, computer firms advertising their wares with free gifts and from enthusiastic teachers dedicated to education and children, seeing what computers can do, wanting to bring the benefits to their work not only to develop the education within a school but also because of the in built need of most educated people to develop and extend their own knowledge and experience.

The problems consequent to this non-organisation will invariably surface if the enthusiast moves on without having institutionalised his work. Expensive equipment may languish in a corner of the school.

The lack of standards and interaction with fellow teachers and the proliferation of odds and ends of equipment making the transfer of software a nightmare are just some of the problems which will mitigate against getting the best value for money from an investment which is not coordinated.

Obviously the new government initiative will go some way to helping in this area but it will still be up to an individual authority how much benefit can be extracted from the net of Regional Information Centres.

Positive

This long introduction brings me to the area that I consider to be the proper role of the LEA, that is one of positive encouragement at whatever level the authority can afford. Even at a minimal level, centralising information, encouraging contacts etc., can have an enormous benefit to the teachers involved by ensuring that they are not alone whilst if an authority can make funds available great steps forward can be made as can be seen at ILEA, Birmingham, Manchester, Derby and possibly Bradford.

I believe that the existence of a 'centre' is essential, this may be simply an advisor, or teacher or could be a number of staff set aside at a local Poly, university, teachers' centre or Computing Centre. Whatever or wherever it is, it provides a local focus for teachers which the new Regional Information Centres, although very welcome, will still not be able to provide.

4.2 BRADFORD'S APPROACH, THE SCHOOLS COMPUTING CENTRE

Back in the mists of time (1967, when I left university) the City of Bradford was about to install its first third generation computer, an ICL 1904 and it was decided from the outset that this was not just a treasurer's machine, but a facility for the whole authority so engineers etc. with their Fortran programs got just as much priority as the payroll and had central expertise on hand in the Computer Division (myself) to facilitate their requirements.

We already had one school teaching computing when the ICL-CES scheme was born and, as well as Bradford teachers attending the course, a member of the Computer Division went along. This was the start of providing a batch system for CESIL. At a special 'twilight' hours class Bradford 6th formers were taught Fortran by myself and another programmer and in the summer term they were presented with 'computing certificates' issued by us! This particular school soon had an online terminal to supplement the batch work, and by providing this twilight class for all sixth formers and teachers, spread the word throughout the City.

At the present time all Bradford's Upper Schools have a terminal connected to the Honeywell Mainframe and some have more than one. All the upper schools have at least one 8K Pet and many have more for example, one school has 2 32K Pets, 2 8K Pets a printer and a floppy disc unit. All the schools do some form of computer education – covering the whole range of 'O' level, CSE, 16+ and 'A' level and also computing for 6th formers through to a 'taster' for all 3rd formers.

They are supported by the Bradford Schools Computing Centre based within the City's Computer Division. The support that teachers get depends to a large extent on themselves but consists of numerous separate integrated facets; a summary is given in the last section.

The Schools Computing team comprises of four computer professionals, a development officer, team leader and 2 programmers. They provide the backup to teachers with a telephone query answering service. They also maintain and augment a comprehensive program library on both the mainframe and the micro, provide and maintain documentation and provide training courses on all aspects of computing.

The advisors themselves have attended computing courses and are also able to spread the word. Again, in these difficult times when teacher mobility is severely curtailed, a great deal of the movement is now solely between our own schools' and teachers are reaping the benefit of a cohesive policy since when they move the same equipment and same programs are available and their central contact and support remains constant.

Finally an argument for the 'centre' being attached to the infamous treasurer's computer section! It seems unlikely that even when the promised golden age dawns, a schools computing centre will be able to employ myriads of staff. Being attached to a large group provides an acceptable alternative. It enables the centre to use the right expert at the right time, thereby providing schools with a superior service to one staffed solely by a few people.

The centre thus has access to experts in specialised fields when these suddenly relate to the needs of schools, for instance, Word Processing. It also provides stability – the centre does not depend totally on the small schools team in that if any of the members leave it is easy to fill the gap with another member of staff with the relevant experience. This does, however, rely on a far-seeing and sympathetic computer manager and on a computer division which realises the importance of educating our young people to provide our computer experts of tomorrow.

4.3 THE ROLES OF A SCHOOLS CENTRE

I believe that more important than the hardware and software backup are the people able and willing to provide advice, assistance and specialised training on request. At Bradford we can give the front line support service because we are part of a large installation with people expert in systems software, microfilming, word processing and commercial systems encompassing tight time schedules, high security, cash receipting, libraries and in a multitude of operational systems.

I see the existence of a centre as being essential to help teachers help themselves. The centre can be based in a polytechnic, university, teachers centre or, as in Bradford, within the local Education Authority in a Computer Section. Each solution has its own benefits but quite often it really depends on the people. Obviously I like Bradford's system and I feel that there are great benefits to teachers in being able to maintain contact with the real commercial world of computing. Because the organisation is large the computer section can give education access to up-to-date facilities as soon as they are commercially viable and provide professional operators continually accustomed to tight time schedules and unable to accept lengthy machine breakdowns.

As well as providing a catalyst and reactive support a centre, if suitably funded, can also look at developments; I would see a centre investigating the BBC machine and VIC 20 and providing access to many of the peripherals so that teachers can gain experience before obtaining them for their own schools.

A centre should set and maintain standards, obtain programs for the library and amend them to conform to the standards. These are also central functions in that they are too expensive in teacher time if done in individual schools.

Up to now most of my discourse has been about helping enthusiasts to progress further and could be done by any outside body, but within an LEA there is also the role of encouraging all schools to accept and teach about new technology.

Whilst not necessarily universally accepted, in Bradford the Council can certainly see the importance of new technology and the impact it is having on school leavers. By encouraging new technology firms such as Microvitec to come to our area we are hoping to revitalise the local economy. A prime aim therefore is to make our school children aware of the chip and to match the requirements of companies expanding in new technology with a suitably educated workforce. By providing a 'modern' education we encourage firms to set up factories in our area.

To encourage the use of microcomputers in a school can be quite difficult. Facilities and training are available for all schools and every school is encouraged to make use of them. In order to develop 'across the curriculum' the advisory service have provided a number of extra machines which are allocated to schools by advisors to encourage work in other areas of the curriculum so getting round the problem of 'the computer' being located in the maths department. Tackling the task through a Local Education Authority by providing compatible equipment, facilitating software exchange, and by providing training courses for teachers we believe we are succeeding.

4.4 CURRENT PROVISION OF COMPUTER FACILITIES FOR BRADFORD SCHOOLS

1.   *General*
      The Bradford Schools Computing Centre provides advice, assistance and training to all the authority's teachers of computing. It maintains a central back up and expert advice to teachers through a telephone service.

2.   *Upper Schools*

2.1   *Schools Administration*
2.1.1 The Pupil Records System contains details of all pupils in the City which schools can access to provide them with numerous administrative lists.
2.1.2 A number of schools use the Computer Timetabling System and its complementary system for Option Block pupil choice structuring.
2.1.3 Many schools make use of the Parent's Evening Timetabling System.

2.2   *Computer Studies*
2.2.1 All schools have access to the batch mainframe system which is supported by a courier van service — unfortunately although this started with a turn round time of 24 hours with the increasing number of users this has deteriorated to over 3 days in some cases.
2.2.2 All schools have a mainframe computer terminal for

      i Administration
      ii Computer Studies (all levels)
      iii Other Subjects

2.2.3 There is a basic provision of one 8K Commodore microcomputer and cassette recorder plus one 32K Commodore microcomputer and a printer if 'A' level work is being undertaken.
      Many schools have supplemented the basic provision with extra computers and/or discs and printers.

2.3   *Other Subjects*
Currently there are specialist subject groups for Microcomputers, History, Computer Studies and Science — the science group has been provided with a 32K computer via the science advisor.

2.4   *Training*
Training is currently on an ad hoc basis and is provided by the Computing Centre with the assistance of practising teachers.

3.   *Middle Schools*
A number of schools have already purchased Commodore equipment through their PTA's and a small number of machines are available for loan to schools identified by the Advisor. A limited amount of support is available in the form of software, advice and assistance.

4.   *Primary Schools*
As yet only one primary school is involved although many are showing interest.

5.   *Special Schools*
A number of special schools have purchased their own Commodore equipment through a mixture of capitation, private funds and PTA's. Support, advice and assistance is available and a number of software projects have been completed by University Students placed at the Computing Centre.

6.   *User Groups*

6.1   *School Computer User Group*
This group meets once a term under the chairmanship of Mr G Browne the Mathematics Advisor, to discuss all aspects of Computer Usage in Schools. All Schools are invited and the other groups report to these meetings.

6.2   *Timetabling*
Dealing exclusively with the problems of School Timetabling by Computer this group under the chairmanship of Mr D Templar (Deputy Head, Eccleshill School) holds regular meetings and training sessions.

6.3   *Adminstration*
The group holds regular meetings and has been particularly active in framing the Upper Schools requirements from the Pupil Nominal Roll System. The chairman of this group is Mr N Milford, Thornton School.

6.4   *Computer Studies*

Set up for teachers teaching Computer Studies this group discusses aspects of the various examinations set and also initiates training for teachers.

6.5   *Microcomputers*

The Micro group is chaired by Mr A Lambert of Ilkiey Grammar School and has meetings at least once a term dealing with the introduction of the microcomputer to the classroom.

6.6   *Subject specialisms*

6.6.1   *History*

Mr M Smith (Oakbank School, Keighley) chairs this small group of History teachers who are investigating the use of computers in History teaching.

6.6.2   *Science*

Dr Schillaker the Science Advisor has initiated this group of Science teachers to look at existing software for science teachers with a view to improving it and also identifying areas for new projects. The Advisor has provided a 32K CBM which is at present located at Beckfoot School.

CHAPTER 5

A national software library

David Walker, Director, Scottish Microelectronic Development Program

---

Cataloguing computer software and other relevant information is inherently a much more difficult task than for books or even the non-book materials commonly found in libraries. The extra dimensions of language dialects, program structures, memory and system and peripheral requirements, lesson and classroom management, educational and technical documentation, transferability and system to system interfacing all contribute to the problem – to say nothing of the difficulties associated with copyright. The phrase 'software library' will be taken as all things to all men. It will be assumed to include systems' software, requiring links with manufacturers and suppliers. Many users will probably not distinguish between program, system software and hardware failures and so debugging and diagnostic test routines will be essential. The library will be regarded as a computer resource centre and people will want to browse, thus creating a need for a selection of the main microcomputer systems currently in use in education and, possibly, a wide range of peripherals. Copiers will be required: not just the normal photocopiers but also magnetic tape and floppy disc copying units and perhaps even EPROM facilities. The comments above certainly pose a large number of difficulties but they should not be regarded as an impregnable barrier – simply as a challenge which must be met.

5.1 LEVELS

It is essential that materials should be held in broad categories. For example, two levels of package (program and all documentation) can be readily identified, the lower consisting of contributed programs and documentation which are available to all but without guarantee. The upper level library would comprise packages considered to be educationally valuable, adequately documented and technically sound and these would be maintained, with guarantees, by the staff in association with the author. Programs from the lower tier, after evaluation by a group of subject specialists, could be selected for further development with a view to inclusion in the upper library. Each level would involve some software bearing acquisition or other costs so that charges to users would result.

Different levels of information would inevitably be held on different packages, from simple, almost self-documented programs to those involving full educational and technical manuals including pupil and teacher notes, subject background, applicability, case studies, listings, hardware and software requirements, details of maintenance procedures, centres of exellence and possible variations in methods and techniques such as multi-user, batch-processing, split-screen options and so on. This subject is expanded upon later.

5.2 LANGUAGE

In Scotland, various computer languages are used in schools and colleges, such as BASIC, PASCAL, FORTRAN, ALGOL, S ALGOL, COBOL, machine code and author languages, Within secondary education, the predominant language is BASIC and this situation will probably continue for several years. Unfortunately, however, as most users of microcomputer systems will have realised, there is no nationally agreed standard for this language, each manufacturer having adopted an individual dialect. Many committees and working parties have been set up to design a standard BASIC for education but, to date, there has been little agreement. Regions and other Authorities, who have used computers in education for some time, are naturally reluctant to accept a standard which would require them to modify all their existing software. Furthermore, strict standardisation would inhibit the exploitation of many specific system characteristics. The lowest common form of BASIC would exclude the use of files, graphics, disc drives, strings and such facilities as voice recognition, light pen, graphics tablets and interfacing devices to external components. Programs cannot, therefore, be transferred freely between different systems. It requires the services of a skilled programmer to spot the dialect differences and modify a program to suit another system. Conditions are further complicated by the current trend of manufacturers to 'improve' their systems in such a way that programs written for their previous models cannot be loaded onto their new systems. Nevertheless, a solution to the BASIC dialect problem is essential to enable good material to be transferred across systems. Authorities, nationally and internationally, should now be putting pressure on microcomputer manufacturers to establish a common version of BASIC. The educational market is large and we in education wish to freely exchange ideas and experiences without having to encounter unnecessary barriers imposed by the manufacturing industry.

Peripherals and applications
Many packages take advantage of specialised peripherals associated with a particular system which makes them inoperable without these devices. Technical

notes and application information must be held on current industrial and commercial activities employing a wide range of peripherals, together with reports on relevant educational applications.

5.3 CLASSROOM MANAGEMENT

The techniques of classroom management vary greatly depending on the quality and quantity of equipment available. The use of a single micro, a group of individual machines or one multi-user system all pose different problems. It is important to have information on approaches which allow an entire class to be involvoled in a lesson assoicated with a single micro and not solely the pupil at the keyboard. Equally, it may be possible to schedule the use so that everyone has some time with the machine. This may be particularly true in subjects containing a practical element. The effects on assessment and record-keeping must be considered and the whole debate of chalk versus the microcomputer should be available for study and discussion. School administration by computer is of growing interest and details of local and national activities should be held to encourage co-operation and to reduce duplication.

Documentation
Information from a software library must be able to be understood by users with a wide variety of computing backgrounds. Authors who are bitten by the programming bug often become engrossed in and fascinated by the coding problems. Once the problems have been solved, the enthusiasts often search for and become involved in further intriguing problems. Like the crossword puzzle enthusiasts, programming addicts see satisfaction in the completion of the problem where the complicated solution processes have developed in the mind and not on paper. However, a computer program without documentation is like a completed crossword puzzle without clues — an achievement to the solver but meaningless to colleagues. Not only is it sometimes difficult to guess the intentions of a program just from using it, but people often want to know about a program at times and places when the appropriate machine may not be available. After all, a disc or cassette cannot be scanned or browsed like a periodical. Good documentation is essential and may involve any of the elements listed under section 5.1. It should help the teacher to understand what the program is about, why the computer is being used in the first place, how the program works, what preparation and follow-up is needed, how it is intended to be used (individual or group work, teacher demonstration) and what is needed to run it (types of micro, memory requirements, any special features). It should also help the pupil while using the machine. For example, if the program embodies screenfuls of text (a practice in itself worth questioning) they should be reproduced in the documentation so that several pupils can read it at their own speed. If a number of values are to be tabulated or recorded, a worksheet could be helpful. If the program is in several

stages, a flow chart or overview may help the student to keep track of where he or she is. If the program is liable to crash or be easily upset, for example by unexpected inputs, it is helpful to point this out (and even better to make the program 'crash-proof'). Documentation can also help learners to get optimum use of precious time on the machine by helping them prepare for it and then follow up the work.

Interfacing

Different microcomputer systems have difficulties in 'speaking' to each other. Some microcomputer systems even have difficulty speaking to their own earlier generation. Not only do BASIC dialects differ between systems but the magnetic storage media are not compatible. For example, mini floppy discs cannot physically be transferred between various manufacturer's microcomputer systems. It is essential that we move towards 'micro speaking unto micro'. The use of the microcomputer as an interface to laboratory experiments is one of the major growth areas in Scotland. It is therefore advisable that software libraries include a section on interfacing circuitry.

5.4 SOURCES OF SOFTWARE

The collection of software for a library poses different problems to those encountered with book libraries. Educational material produced by commercial software houses does not exist in any great volume. The bulk of good educational software will come from educationalists, although such material may eventually be polished up by commercial houses, particularly with regard to documentation presentation. In a country the size of Scotland there are literally thousands of programs written by teachers and lecturers. Most of these will be 20 to 40 lines in length, written to solve a very specific problem. A national library should endeavour to encourage all such programs to be submitted. Even short programs can be useful to stimulate new ideas or can point the user towards the solution of a particular problem. Authors have to be encouraged to submit their work. Experience has shown that authors working in the more remote areas of Scotland, having no direct access to the larger working groups, do not appreciate the potential of their own work. Although the ultimate goal is a polished package comprising the program and educational and technical documentation, authors should be encouraged to submit their work with or without documentation in the first instance. The collection of software is often a missionary exercise but the results can be highly rewarding.

5.5 DISTRIBUTION

New methods of distribution will have to be developed for computer software. No one library could attend the needs of Scotland and so a network, possibly hierarchical, is required. A national centre interchanging internationally on one hand and with regional and local centres on the other would be ideal. Operating on the two-tier system outlined earlier, it would make available, without guarantee everything contained in the lower level but all material in the upper cataolgue would be totally maintained. The regional centres would employ a similar system, actively sending top-tier material to the national centre, where it might be accessed by other regions or by international agencies, and collecting new packages locally for the lower level with a view to evaluation and possible development later.

The day-to-day running of such libraries would require considerable thought. Should they issue single copies or class-sets of documentation? On-site reproduction of programs and materials would cause bottlenecks but preduplication could have massive storage and staffing implications. Documentation might be transferred by disc but this would have the effect of moving the bottleneck from the library to the user-site.

5.6 CONCLUSION

The establishment of a national software library with international links is an essential element in the development of microcomputing in education. The problem is expense. The cost of duplication of effort is never quantified but the cost of national and associated regional centres has been and is certainly large. But the interchange of ideas and experiences within a country and across local and national boundaries is a social, educational and economic necessity. The intention of this article is not to discourage agencies from establishing a national centre but to highlight the nature of the problems and the scale of the effort required. Software libraries require local and national funding, and with some urgency, before we become too introverted either locally or nationally.

CHAPTER 6

Microcomputers and special education: survey and prospects

Peter Goodyear and Annette Barnard, Aston University

6.1 PREAMBLE – A ROLE FOR ACADEMIC RESEARCH

In a rapidly moving field, such as that created by the impact of microelectronics on education, it is inevitable that there should exist, at any one time, a great deal of variation in levels of experience and understanding. While some debate the finer points of machine architecture or talk nonchalently of RAMs, bugs and glitches others struggle with more wordly matters – 'what will it cost?', 'will the kids break it?', 'can I learn BASIC in a free period?'. This diversity of expertise (and corresponding demand for information) threatens to deepen the already unfathomable chasm separating academic researchers from the teachers who actually have to hew away at the 'chalk face'. If the majority of teachers in Special Education currently want to know whether to buy an Apple or a PET what are we doing talking about Artificial Intelligence and software mounted only on IBM mainframes? Our answer to this is simplistic. Academic researchers have three resources in substantially greater quantity than practising teachers:

(1) They have easy access to relatively vast computing facilities;
(2) They have a well articulated network of information sources;
(3) Above all else, they have the time to look up from their everyday work and survey the horizon for promising developments.

This is not to imply that researchers in educational computing should dissociate themselves from the work actually going on in the classroom – quite the reverse. What we would argue is that if they fail to take advantage of the three sets of resources with which they are blessed then they are also failing in this responsibility to teachers and to the kids. The business of advising the novice on existing software and hardware should be (and is coming to be) undertaken by a whole range of agencies and individuals – local teacher networks, user groups, LEA advisers, the new MEP regional centres, the Council for Educational Technology and units like CEDAR at Imperial College, London.

All this is a prologue to saying that the present paper is not solely concerned with current applications of PET microcomputers in Special Education. Rather the paper will:

(1) Briefly categorise and comment upon current work using microcomputers with learners who have special educational needs.

(2) Even more briefly outline the likely impact of the government's Micro-electronics Education Programme (MEP) on Special Education.

(3) Describe the *style* of educational computing which our project at Aston University sees as paying the greatest dividends.

The Aston project, which is still in its infancy, draws upon some fairly demanding work in Artificial Intelligence and is therefore furthest removed from what can now be done using microcomputers. However, as the real cost of microcomputer power diminishes, the prospect of applying such work routinely in the classroom becomes even more real. One of the functions of user groups such as this should be to articulate demands on manufacturers for the facilities our educational work so sorely needs.

6.2 SURVEY AND TYPOLOGY

There exists a number of possibilities for classifying the use of microcomputer technology in Special Education. The type of problem experienced by the child might be taken as a taxonomic criterion — such that work with the deaf or the blind or the autistic might each be subsumed under a separate heading. Altern-atively, significance might be attached to the mode of use of the microcomputer, whether as a communication aid, or in conventional CAL, for example. Yet again, organisational characteristics of the work might be important — is it an individual school initiative or a larger collaborative project?, located in a Special School or a remedial department?, does it use home-produced software or only bought-in products?

For the purposes of this survey a four-fold typology will be used. This is derived from the Council for Educational Technology's summary of ways in which microelectronics (broader than microcomputers) might be used to help children with special educational needs (CET, 1981, 9-13). These are:

(1) The microcomputer as a diagnostic aid.
(2) The microcomputer as a learning environment.
(3) The microcomputer as a communication aid.
(4) The microcomputer as a provider of feedback.

As with most classification these categories are neither mutually exclusive nor exhaustive.

The microcomputer as a diagnostic aid

While the microcomputer cannot, and should not, replace the teacher as judge of a child's learning needs, a combination of educational and psychological testing tools with microcomputer technology might greatly assist in the diagnosis of learning problems. The use of computer-based educational testing systems is well-advanced (for example, Rushby, 1979, 52–75; McMahon, 1978; Bladon and Bailey, 1981). However, a number of factors currently militate against the use of the microcomputer as a diagnostic aid and the CET investigation of 1979/80 found no evidence of its use in this role in the UK, (CET, 1981, 9). On a limited scale, some programs exist at Walshall Education Development Centre, for testing the basic mathematical skills of ESN (M) children (Hart and Staples, 1980).

The microcomputer as a learning environment

The bulk of applications in this field are what might be called 'conventional CAL'. For the most part they are centred on specific, relatively small-scale teaching programs — often home-written — which offer remedial help with (typically) language and mathematical skills. Language programs range from letter or word matching, through the fitting of short sentences to pictures, to fairly sophisticated applications aiding sentence construction. Examples of fairly simple but effective vocabulary-building software, which tap the motivational capacities of computer-based games, are to be found in adaptable 'Hangman-type' programs such as those in use with PETs at Anthony Gell School, Derbyshire and the Hamble School, Southampton (for instance, Clamp, 1981); Ian Staples, of Jane Lane School, Walsall, has developed an ingenious written-story-to-picture matching program using an adaptable input device. The main thrust of work aimed at improving sentence-construction and related written language skills would appear to be directed at the deaf and partially hearing. Of particular interest is a project at Hull University led by Dr A. B. Rostron (Sewell, *et al.,* 1980).

Conventional CAL programs dealing with basic mathematical skills are growing rapidly in quantity, particularly for ESN (M) children. Myra Duffy (1981) describes eleven testing, demonstration and practice programs developed in Coventry as part of an attempt to computerise work around very clearly defined behavioural objectives. At the same level, maths programs associated with a coin-input keyboard (see below) are being written at the Walsall Education Development Centre (Hart and Staples 1980), and are also in use in remedial work at Benjamen Britten High School, Lowestoft and Anthony Gell School, Wirksworth (Avis and Parry, 1981). Finally, an interesting, though only partly successful attempt at teaching BASIC programming to maladjusted boys as a method for exploring mathematics is reported by Cox (1981) of Surrey University.

The United States and Canada have something of a lead on Britain in the use of microcomputers in the education of children with special learning needs. The availability of cheap colour graphs has been a significant incentive for the adoption of computer assisted learning in US schools for the deaf. Von Feld (1978) offers a nation-wide picture of computer applications in schools for the deaf while interesting insights into the work of individual schools can be obtained from such sources as Hoffmeyer (1980) and Arcanin and Zawolkow (1980). The Calgary based survey of Hallworth and Brebner (1978) provides an overview of American projects involving the mentally handicapped and Paul Goldenberg's *Special Technology for Special Children* contains a number of original perspectives which counterbalance the dominant American tradition of 'Skinnerian' CAI.

The microcomputer as a communication aid

Communication aids can be divided into two categories — those which use a microcomputer to help the handicapped person communicate with the outside world and those which facilitate the learner's communication with the micro-computer itself. The first, more general, application is not of direct relevance here though mention should be made of microcomputer enhancements to existing Possum-type devices (as in the work of Ian Glen at Brays School, Birmingham) and of micropressor-exploiting hardware for the blind such as the Optacon. Further information can be obtained from the newsletter ACE (Aids, Communication and Electronics) produced by P Odor in Edinburgh or from Helen Townley, organiser of the British Computer Society's 'DEARS' project.

QWERTY keyboards and small VDUs are far from optimal mechanisms when it comes to communication between (even unhandicapped) learners and educational microcomputers. Consequently, a great deal of effort has gone into adapting input and output devices to meet special needs. Variations on Bit-Pads, Glen's 'concept keyboard', the Walsall 'primary keyboard' (Hart and Staples, 1980), joysticks, suck/blow switches and foot controls are being developed in profusion. Particularly popular for input to mathematics programs involving money has been an adapted calculator keyboard with a coin of each denomination replacing the number buttons. A simple modification of this device for the PET is described by Avis and Parry (1981) and in Chapter 13.

Output to VDUs needs to be designed in a particularly clear fashion for work in the Special Education context. Good use can be made of even low-resolution graphics facilities, and routines are available for generating enlarged character output for those with poor vision. In American schools for the deaf considerable progress is being made in interfacing microcomputers with other serial or random access visual media — videotape, videodisk and still slide, for example (see Cronin, *et al.*, 1979; Fox, 1979; Galbraith, *et al.*, 1979). Of course output need not be to a VDU and some of the more interesting work with younger learners utilises programmable robots such as the LOGO 'turtle' (Papert, 1980a and see below).

Finally, mention should be made of developments in synthetic voice output for blind users of CAL material. Of promise in this area is the Open University's research on microcomputer based voice synthesisers (Vincent, 1981).

The microcomputer as a provider of feedback

Microcomputer based systems have considerable potential as providers of instant feedback for children with special learning difficulties. This is particularly true in the exercise of specific perceptual and motor skills. For example, the popular press have enthusiastically reported the potential of computer video games for those with motor difficulties and also for autistic children. The computer's motivational power, but also the *consistency* of its response to the child's actions, would appear to account for a large part of its success (CET, 1981, 12). Hart and Staples (1980) also mention the value of animated graphic maze games for tackling the problem of directional confusion.

This brief survey of recent developments in certain areas of microcomputer assisted special education is by no means exhaustive; rather its purpose is to give an indication of the main trend in explorations of the microcomputer's educational capabilities. This will serve as a backdrop for the project to be described in the penultimate section of this paper. Before that, it may be useful to offer a short summary of the government's Microelectronics Education Programme (MEP) as it affects Special Education.

6.3 THE MEP/CET SPECIAL EDUCATION PROGRAMME

Following the launching of the MEP with its celebrated £9 million, the Council for Education Technology submitted (in March 1981) a proposal for £1.1 million of funding for work in Special Education (CET, 1981).

By July 1981 the MEP's Advisory Committee had agreed that money could be provided for the exploration and development of seven key areas.[†]

    (1) The funding of regional curriculum development groups, coming together through the LEA's, as envisaged in the MEP's *Strategy* document. A maximum of £120,000 pa with possible £30,000 pa for 'one off' projects.

    (2) 11 one-week teacher training courses over three years.

    (3) The establishment of 4 'Special Education Microelectronic Resource Centres' (SEMERC's) in parallel with the MEP's 14 Regional Centres. Each to have a regional role but also a specialism in:

    (a) the blind

    (b) the deaf and language impaired (including dyslexia)

    (c) the physically handicapped

    (d) ESN(S) and autistic children.

£16,000 per centre pa plus an initial £30,000 per centre for equipment and books.

[†]We are indebted to Mrs Mary Hope, Council for Educational Technology, for providing this information.

(4) £10,000 pa for consultancy on communication aids.

(5) £47,000 for two special investigations into

(a) the problems of access of physically handicapped and blind learners to CAL material

(b) the development of input devices for severely handicapped children.

(6) The production of a Special Education issue of ACE to go to all special schools in Autumn 1981.

(7) £20,000 for the production of small devices for educational applications which would not otherwise be economically feasible.

Rapid progress is expected with regard to the establishment of the four SEMERC's and a final decision on their geographical location in anticipated before the date of the Pet Ed Conference. In addition it has recently been announced that the West Midlands MEP Regional Centre (under the direction of Ian Glen) is to have a particular responsibility for Special Education. Despite the official obsession with British-made microcomputers, PET-lovers will be glad to learn that the West Midlands Centre *will* be supporting their favourite beast.

6.4 CONTAINMENT OF AN INNOVATION?

£9 million is not a great deal of money to be shared across the educational community. However, it *is* bound to make an impact and will be of considerable assistance to teachers and Local Authority advisers active in educational computing. The prospects for extending current work look good. But therein lies the rub. Of necessity the MEP has been forced to erect a very well-defined framework within which it can judge whether certain sorts of educational computing activity (inter alia) can be supported from its funds. This legitimating framework had to be assembled quickly and, once assembled, it has to be static — otherwise nobody knows where they stand. Unfortunately, the worlds of microelectronics and computer science are extremely dynamic. Hence in supporting styles of microcomputer usage going on in schools at the moment, the MEP strategy is in danger of ossifying current practice. This would be worrying enough in itself but we believe that this potential check to growth may have come at a singularly unfortunate time. To convince you of this, we need to develop two arguments.

First, we believe there to be two fundamentally contradictory movements in educational computing, two *styles* of using the computer as an educational tool. The older tradition is the one which at present dominates in schools. It has its roots in Skinner and programmed learning and is epitomised in American Stimulus-Response CAI software. British software developed from the early 1970s onwards has been (mercifully) less behaviourist but, for the most part, not fundamentally different in kind. It is still essentially *teacher-centred*. That is, it takes as its model the activities of a classroom teacher – presenting information, testing, supervising drill-and-practice, keeping marks.

Against this there exists a second tendency, which might be called *child-centred*. This takes as its model the child as a naturally able and insatiable learner and attempts to develop combinations of software and hardware which allow the child to use the computer as a powerful tool with which to explore and manipulate the world. Seymour Papert (1980a, 5) nicely distinguishes the two opposing tendencies as 'the computer programming the child' and 'the child programming the computer'. At present, most of the 'child-centred' work manifests itself as what is called research (it is led by university workers not the schoolteachers, uses relatively large computing facilities and draws on the methods of Artificial Intelligence).

Our second argument concerns the practicalities surrounding the adoption in schools of an innovation like the microcomputer. It centres on a belief that containment of an innovation is a well-polished talent of the educational system. Partly, this rests on teachers and the limits to the time and energy they can spend on coping with new developments. A certain number of them, whether out of educational conviction or ambition, have taken the time to learn about and introduce microcomputers in their teaching. They have learnt BASIC, written programs and cajoled their colleagues into buying hardware and CAL packages. Having expended this energy they feel due some respite, and perhaps a little respect. They cannot keep on running in a fruitless attempt not to lose sight of the leading edge of computing R and D. Hence there settles an orthodoxy on educational computing such as we have at the moment. True there are little sprints and challenges – BASIC or COMAL?, Acorns or PETs? – but nobody should venture too far or the whole field will have to restart the marathon.

The danger is that this orthodoxy, reinforced by the MEP, has established itself just in time to block out 'child-centred' developments in educational computing. Furthermore there is the risk of a backlash. Popular and governmental enthusiasm for microelectronics was borne in on a spate of evangelising books, articles and television programmes which made many a bold claim for the powers of the microcomputer. The MEP was funded amidst this enthusiasm. By resting too early in the race to fulfill those bold claims there is engendered a distinct possibility that microcomputer technology (in education, as elsewhere) will be accused of not coming up with the goods. That should see an end to funding.

Special Education and child-centred computing

It is difficult to argue that spending large sums of money on drawing out the educational applicability of Artificial Intelligence research would be sufficient to emancipate children from teacher-centred educational computing. As Papert argues (1980b) there are strong socio-political forces which favour the current pedagogical model. Quite possibly child-centred educational computing will come about first in the home rather than in the classroom (and the middle-class home at that). But Special Education is slightly different, if only because the emancipation of handicapped kids is less socio-politically threatening. With this in mind, the next section outlines our project at Aston.

6.5 FOUNDATIONS OF THE ASTON PROJECT

At the heart of our philosophy of educational computing lies a belief, shared with Papert (1980a), that children are gifted at learning and that much of what currently occurs in schools deforms this gift. Computers, used in the right way (as powerful tools), can extend childrens' natural learning capacities by giving them an enhanced ability to manipulate and explore the real (and other) world(s). That microtechnology can help compensate those with special learning difficulties in this same fashion should be self-evident.

Papert's LOGO work uses the computer to provide children with the materials whereby they can readily build their own intellectual structures in the particular domain of mathematics. The computer compensates for the poverty of our mathophobic culture in such building materials (*ibid*, 7). Physically handicapped children are similarly but doubly deprived. Not only is their culture deficient in this vital intellectual building material but they, in their individual lives, are further blocked off from such material by their disabilities.

One obvious corollary of this line of thought, which we are following up at Aston, is that LOGO's system of 'turtle-graphics' offers a very visual approach to mathematical learning which by-passes some of the language handicaps of the deaf.

Turning a computer into a powerful tool which can be used by a child (whether or not he is classified as having special educational needs) to build his own intellectual structures needs a different sort of software development programme from that typical of most work going on in educational computing at the moment. The emphasis shifts from software which, broadly speaking, simulates the teacher, to software which allows the child to become what we conventionally regard as a researcher (in kind, if not degree). That is, in Papert's phrase, the child is not taught mathematics but rather he becomes a mathematician.

Design of the educational computing system needed to allow this falls into four parts:

(1) A powerful central software component consisting of one or more of: natural language processor/ simulation program/ special language/ pattern recogniser/ modelling package/ database manipulator/ . . . etc.
(2) Software to act as an adaptable 'ultra-user-friendly' interface between (1) and the child.
(3) Software and hardware to cope with the child's specific learning handicaps (for instance, special input devices).
(4) Hardware elements with the capacity to mount (1) to (3).

Outline of a design for a written-language exploring system

Papert's work at MIT, using LOGO in mathematics education, represents only one possibility for allowing children access to powerful computing resources. (Incidentally, 'turtle-graphics' are becoming available on microcomputers; notably the Terak, Apple II and Research Machines 380Z). In the same way that manipulating a 'turtle' can stimulate exploration of mathematical concepts and problem-solving strategies so, we believe, the computer can be harnessed to the task of aiding children with written language difficulties. Numerous projects (for example, Ian Staple's work at Jane Lane School, mentioned above) make good use of animated computer graphics in remedial reading work. It seems feasible not only that animated graphics could be used in the area of *writing* skills but that their use in writing, rather than reading, comes closer to the desideratum of using computers to increase childrens' power over the world around them. This inverts the current relationship between words and pictures characteristic of current computer-based remedial literacy schemes. At present, systems are teacher-centred rather than child-centred; the child is shown a picture of a cat on the VDU and responds by pressing or typing the word 'CAT' on the input device. At a basic level, a *child*-centred words-to-pictures system would accept the word ('CAT' or whatever) from the child and would respond with a picture of a cat. Building up from individual words to phrases and sentences would evoke more complex graphics; action would produce animation. In this way the computer lends power to the child, in his learning, by amplifying the effect on the immediate world around him of his use of the written word. (This is close to John Seely Brown's concept of 'computer animation as a *reactive* medium for creative expression' – Brown (1977, 255) our emphasis).

Storing graphic images to mirror nouns would seem to be a technically trivial if potentially large task. But how feasible is it to suggest providing animated images which will respond to phrases and more complex grammatical constructs? Research in Artificial Intelligence and Computational Linguistics in the area known as 'natural language processing' suggests that the problems are not intractable. Take the work of Terry Winograd (1972). Winograd's system involved a robot ('SHRDLU') which responded to written natural language inputs by moving blocks of different shapes and colours around on a table. It also responded with written output to clarify its actions (or 'understanding') or to ask for extra information. By having a clear internal representation of the very limited world in which it was operating. SHRDLU could display an impressive 'grasp' of natural language – including the ability to cope with passives, act on commands phrased as questions and relate the meaning of words like 'it' and 'that' back to previous statements. A command such as 'Pick up the big red block' presents no difficulties at all but SHRDLU could even tackle nested horrors like 'Does the shortest thing the tallest pyramid's supports support anything green?'

Other strands of research parallel Winograd's, and perhaps go beyond it. An appropriate example can be found in the Yale University SAM system described by Schank and Lehnert (1979) — a system designed with the capacity to 'understand, make inferences from, and answer questions on' short English language stories or 'scripts', a typical example being a visit to a restaurant.

Natural language processors like these depend, to an extent, on the quantity of 'background knowledge' built into them. This means that most of them work when they are handling fairly narrow areas of life; fairly narrow 'domains' such as Winograd's Blockworld or SAM's outing to a restaurant. Does this not impose unacceptable limits on the freedom of written expression allowed to children using the putative system? Possibly this is so, but it raises two interesting points.

Firstly, it may be fruitful to return to Papert's work using LOGO, where childrens' activity in programming the computer to execute its 'turtle-graphics' is described *to them* as 'teaching the turtle'. If the child wants the turtle to move in a clockwise circle he sees himself as 'teaching the turtle' or 'teaching the system' how to execute a circle. Could there not be a corresponding activity in our written language system?†

Secondly, it is possible to build domain constraints into an individual application of the system without violating the child's feeling of creative freedom — by, in a sense, setting a topic for the child's story. Writing a description of a house, for example, would draw on a much smaller repertoire of words and grammatical constructs (and need a much smaller 'background knowledge' database) than is called up by the SAM system.

The problem of domain constraint also leads us into the consideration of (non-VDU) output or display hardware, since the use of a robot to respond to the child's written input brings in its own constraints. For example, the language of movement associated with Papert's LOGO turtle is a domain constrained very largely by the characteristics of the output medium.

There are other possibilities for robot-type output. One which we are thinking about at Aston is based on an inversion of Tony Blagg's 'Blaggsville' (Walsall EDC again). 'Blaggsville' is a model village mounted on a base-board which is slotted to a allow a figure to be manually moved (by the child) through the village streets. Electric switches located at junction points and landmarks in the village are triggered when the figure is moved past them. The sequence of switching is passed to a microcomputer which interprets the figure's movements as the story of a journey. At the conclusion, the written story is output, complete with computer-stored illustrations.

An inversion of this system, which gives more power to the child's attempts with the written word, would involve a robot figure moving about the board (village streets) in response to the results of a computer 'interpretation' of the child's written story input. The setting, 'Blaggsville' or wherever, provides a

---

†Most natural language processing systems have facilities for 'teaching' the system new words. As an illustration of how this sort of facility can be deployed in primary school written language see Sharples (1981).

limit to the range of possibilities which the child can incorporate in his story, thereby helping constrain the domain which the natural language processing system must cope with. The relationship between the output device and other components of the system hardware and software are schematised in Fig. 6.1.

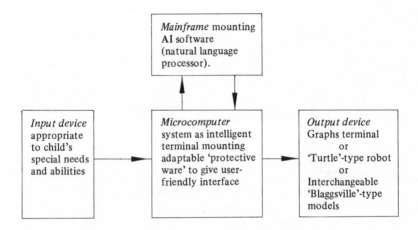

Fig. 6.1 — A possible architecture for the written-language exploring system.

The next stage in our planning of the system will be an analysis of the capabilities of selected existing natural language processors to see which most closely fits with the task of improving written language skills.

6.6 CONCLUSION FOR THE FUTURE

The main point of this paper has been to argue that educational users of the PET (and other microcomputers) must not take what is currently done using micros (however valuable) as any kind of guide to what will be possible in the very near future. The dangers of a creeping orthodoxy, containing an extremely conservative view of educational computing, need to be identified and resisted. One way of maintaining a healthy dynamism in educational practice is to follow, and think about the educational potential of, developments in such exciting areas as Natural Language Processing and Expert Systems. Researchers active in educational computing must play a part in channelling ideas and information (in both directions). In the day-to-day routine of the classroom it is too easy for demoralisation to set in, and for the limitations of currently affordable microcomputing systems to constrain our imaginations. Children with special educational needs deserve the biggest ideas we can muster.

REFERENCES

Arcanin, J. and Zawolkow, G., (1980), 'Microcomputers in the service of students and teachers: CAI at the California School for the Deaf', *Am. Ann. Deaf*, 125, 807-13.

Avis, P. and Parry, S., (1981), 'A coin-input keyboard for the PET', *Input-Output*, 1.

Bladon, P. and Bailey, R., (1981), 'Monitoring student progress with the aid of a computer', *Bull. Ed. Res.*, 21, 17-26.

Brown, J. S., (1977), 'Uses of artificial intelligence and advanced computer technology in education, 253-70 in Seidel, R. and Rubin, M., *Computers and communication: implications for education*, Academic Press, London.

C. E. T., (1981), *Microelectronics and children with special educational needs*, Council for Educational Technology, London.

Clamp, S., (1981), 'C. A. L. with secondary 'remedials' – eighteen months on', *Input-Output*, 1.

Cox, M., (1981), *A trial course in BASIC programming and mathematics using CAL for a group of maladjusted boys*, paper at CAL 81, Leeds.

Cronin, B., *et al.*, (1979), 'DAVID system: the development of an interactive video system at the National Technical Institute for the Deaf', *Am. Ann. Deaf*, 124, 616-23.

Duffy, M., (1981), 'Programs to reinforce behavioural objectives', *Input-Output*, 3.

Fox, R., (1979), 'Computer controlled interactive motion and still image film projection system for vocational education for the deaf', *J. Ed. Tech. Syst.*, 7, 3, 229-37.

Galbraith, G., *et al.*, (1979), 'Interfacing an inexpensive home computer to the videodisc: educational implications for the hearing-impaired', *Am. Ann. Deaf*, 124, 536-41.

Goldenberg, P., (1979), *Special technology for special children*, University Park Press, Baltimore.

Hallworth, H. and Brebner, A., (1978), *Computer assisted instruction and the mentally handicapped: some recent developments*, paper to Assoc. for Ed. Data Systems, Atlanta.

Hart, B. and Staples, I., (1980), 'Microcomputers in Special Schools', *Special Education: Forward Trends*, 7, 4.

Hoffmeyer, D., (1980), 'Computer-aided instruction at the Florida School for the Deaf and Blind', *Am. Ann. Deaf*, 125, 834-40.

Klix, F., (1979), *Human and artificial intelligence*, Elsevier, North Holland.

McMahon, H., (1978), 'Progress and prospects in computer managed learning in the UK', *Programmed Learning and Educational Technology*, 15, 2, 104-13.

Papert, S., (1980a), *Mindstorms: children, computers and powerful ideas*, Harvester Press, Brighton.

Papert, S., (1980b), 'Computers and learning', 73-86 in Dertouzos, M. and Moses, J., *The Computer Age,* MIT Press.
Rushby, N., (1979), *An introduction to educational computing,* Croom Helm, London.
Schank, R. and Lehnert, J., (1979), Computer understanding of stories, 135-40 in Klix, (1979).
Sewell, D., *et al.,* (1980), 'Language and the deaf: an interactive microcomputer based approach', *Brit. J. Ed. Tech.,* 11, 1, 57-68.
Sharples, M., (1981), 'A computer written language lab', *Computer Education,* 37, 10-12.
Vincent, T., (1981), *Computer assisted support for blind students,* paper at CAL 81, Leeds.
Von Feld, J., (1978), 'National survey of the use of computer assisted instruction in schools for the deaf', *J. Ed. Tech. Syst.,* 7, 1, 29-38.
Winograd, T., (1972), *Understanding natural language,* Academic Press, New York.

CHAPTER 7

COMAL – an educational alternative

Borge Christensen, States Training College, Tonder, Denmark

7.1 PROBLEMS WITH BASIC

God created the computer to make life easier and more diverting to man. Shortly after, the Devil invented BASIC to confuse man's mind and make it harder for him to use computers. He did this using some of his favourite tricks. To begin with his Dark Majesty's suggestions always looks very attractive and – above all – very convenient! But later on, when people have been trapped, life gradually turns difficult and confusing to them.

In his latest book *Mindstorms* Seymour Papert says,

> An example of BASIC ideology is the argument that BASIC is easy to learn because it has a very small vocabulary. . . Its small vocabularly can be learned quickly enough. But using it is a different matter. Programs in BASIC acquire so labyrinthine a structure that in fact only the most motivated and brilliant ('mathematical') children do learn to use it for more than trivial ends.

In 1973 we had to face a problem at the States Training College, Tonder, Denmark. Since 1972 we had taught computer science to the maths students. At first everybody was happy. Miles of programs were written and run. But the winter of our discontent was near, as it appeared. After a short start most students went away from the computer, sullenly murmuring something about 'dumb machine' or 'nothing but silly error messages'. A few freaks worked on, however, and that soon gave rise to another problem. An unoffending teacher might sit for hours to decode a nitty-gritty program written by some eager soul, perhaps ending up concluding that a substantial percentage of the program lines might just as well be left out since they were never executed anyhow. Gradually we realised that Shakespeare was right. Something was rotten in the State of Denmark.

Only this time it was not the Danes. So we had to find out what else could be wrong. By some coincidence I came to talk to Benedict Lofstedt at the Department of Computer Science, University of Aarhus, about our problems, and he convinced me that the only thing really rotten in this case was the programming language. The language, he claimed, was seriously and fundamentally defective. He advised me to look in some new book called *Systematic Programming* by one Niklaus Wirth.

That book appeared to be a true revelation. Nobody who knows just a little about computers and programming and has not had his language center totally ruined by using flowcharts and BASIC can be left unaffected or may be even a little shocked by seeing how simple and yet powerful a programming language can be. It was all there, and from then on it has been quite clear to me that BASIC may be a proper code for calculations but that it is most certainly not a higher programming language. I would like to quote Papert again,

> There are also the computerists, the people in the computer world who make decisions about what languages their computers will speak. These people, generally engineers, find BASIC quite easy to learn, partly because they are accustomed to learning such very technical systems and partly because BASIC's sort of simplicity appeals to their system of values.

The language of *Systematic Programming* is Pascal, and the virtues of Pascal are obvious though it was not a very well known language in 1974 and did not have the reputation it has today. But even so there is another important aspect in the case of Pascal against BASIC. In Pascal you have to learn how to use a text editor to input or change programs; in BASIC line numbers are used to replace and delete program statements as well as to sequence them. If your BASIC has a screen editor at its disposal it is easy to 'walk around' on the screen and make minor modifications, adjusting printouts etc. In Pascal you also need to learn a separate Operating System command language to specify different modes of operation. BASIC has its own set of simple commands (LIST, RUN, SAVE etc.) which refer in an obvious way to the program in workspace or on some external device.

Features like the ones mentioned above and many more are often used to defend BASIC against Pascal, but they do in fact not relate to the programming languages as such, but rather to the *operating environment* in which they are used. They are, however, very important and may even be crucial to the non-professional user. On the whole I would say that the environment of the programming language – its human interface – is a highly important, but very often deplorably neglected aspect of a computer system.

Our BASIC lived in a very convenient operating environment: it was a fully interactive, multi-user system with good file handling and we needed all that. But it still was a much too poor language to go on using, so what could we do?

7.2 THE ORIGIN OF COMAL

We analysed the situation carefully and came to the conclusion that we might try to improve BASIC rather than replacing it, and Benedict Lofstedt — who is a real computer specialist — suggested that we design a few powerful extensions to our system using some Pascal concepts: long variable names, a global IF-THEN-ELSE (not the one line IF-THEN-ELSE that comes with any silly BASIC nowadays), REPEAT- and WHILE-loops, a multi-branching CASE-structure, and named subroutines. The details were designed during the following six months and in June, 1974, we started to implement the facilities on top of the mini computer BASIC (Data General XBASIC) that we had at our disposal. I coined the word COMAL (COMmon Algorithmic Language) to name the extensions we had planned. The first versions of COMAL were launched in February 1975.

I am not going to expose the details of COMAL on this occasion, but I shall to some extent explain about one of the structures and the thoughts behind it, because that ought to display the main line of ideas that went into the design. I think you agree with me that in setting up a program to solve a certain problem, branchings are the hardest to get right, and more so if nested branchings must be applied. It is no coincidence that to many people 'computer logic' is more or less tantamount to branching — 'a computer can make decisions' —. Let us look at the following picture of a process:

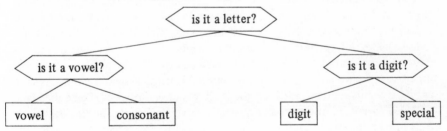

The analysis and solving of the problem may be hard enough, but if that has been done properly the programming language should not be another obstacle on the stony road to a running program. In BASIC you will have to use a very awkward 'upside down' kind of logic to program the process:

```
     IF "it is NOT a letter" THEN xx
     IF "it is a vowel" THEN yy
     PRINT "it is a consonant"
     GOTO zz
yy   PRINT "it is a vowel"
     GOTO zz
xx   IF "it is a digit" THEN pp
     PRINT "it is a special"
     GOTO zz
pp   PRINT "it is a digit"
zz   . . .
```

Well, am I right? Does that mess really work? Is a language like that a proper vehicle to guide the thoughts of those young people who are going to pay for your pension some happy day?

The 'one line IF-THEN-ELSE' so many BASICs are bragging about is not going to do the job much better. You will have to introduce a true multi-line structure to make it simple and straightforward to program:

```
IF "it is a letter" THEN
    IF " is a vowel" THEN
        PRINT "it is a vowel"
    ELSE
        PRINT "it is a consonant"
    ENDIF
ELSE //not a letter//
    IF "it is a digit" THEN
        PRINT "it is a digit"
    ELSE
        PRINT "it is a special"
    ENDIF
ENDIF
```

You do not have to think about line numbers and the strange kind of 'look ahead' that comes from using line numbers as labels. And you do not have to twist the logic the way it is done in the BASIC program. Now add to all this that COMAL interpreters automatically supply the indentation to make the structures appear. The experiences we have had since 1975 indicate above any doubt that we were right in designing and implementing this structure. As soon as the students and the teachers got it they started to use it. Some details in COMAL have been discussed and questioned over the years. This one never was. It is also quite interesting to see that the WATERLOO BASIC has exactly the same construction (only they made theirs in 1978). How painful is it then to see the BBC 'Folks-BASIC' without this fundamental structure. When amateurs design a language they should at least take the trouble to look at designs which have solved one or two fundamental representation problems.

Another important detail in COMAL is the named subroutines. A statement like

```
GOSUB 2000
```

may be understood properly by a computer system, whereas it is absolutely unintelligible to a human processor. Why not make it comprehensive to both man and computer by using a statement like

```
EXEC PRINTOUT
```

You may start arguing: should it be EXEC or should it be CALL?. That I think is a mere matter of taste, as long as it is *clear* what is going on. On introducing the named subroutines and the long variable names we were guided by the principle: Always try to give proper names to objects and processes! After all, what did man start to do as soon as God had blown an immortal soul into him?

7.3 DEVELOPMENT OF COMAL

The impact of COMAL has been stronger than we had guessed that it would be. The students write much better programs than they used to do in BASIC, and their programs have become readable. In general students were much faster than teachers to see that a good tool had come into their hands, but quite soon the attitude of teachers changed in favour of the concept. Since 1977/78 it has become very difficult to sell a BASIC-computer to a school in Denmark.

In 1979 I defined a new version of COMAL to be implemented on a microcomputer. This version — COMAL 80 — was further improved by a working group of academics and representatives of microcomputer manufacturers. COMAL 80 includes such facilities as parameter passing (both value and reference), local variables, and recursion. It has been implemented on the CBM computers — softloaded or hardwired — and on two Danish-made ones. It has been reported to me that implementations on other micros are being made in Ireland, but right now I do not know all the details about these projects.

It can not surprise anybody that COMAL was mainly used for educational purposes. After all, that was what it was meant for. It has been used to teach students about computers and programming, but it has had a even greater use as a tool to write CAI courseware. I shall briefly report on these two aspects:

In computer science the use of COMAL has made it possible for us to change the training strategy radically. As long as you work with BASIC the programs will have to be short and very often unrealistically simple, because the students must write all of it themselves. A library of BASIC programs is not of much use when you want to teach programming. Students cannot learn from other peoples' BASIC programs, simply because it is almost impossible to make them easy to read; the word encoding is usually the proper one to apply to BASIC source programs. A well-written COMAL program on the other hand is self explanatory — just like a good Pascal program used to be. So instead of having the majority of the students wasting their time trying to type very slowly some four line BASIC program, we start them up on programs that have been made ready for them beforehand and stored on the disk. Typically they start to read and analyse a program, and then they are asked to modify and extend it to serve them better. They learn the details of the programming language and at the same time classical algorithms and the style of experienced programmers. After each series of lessons they are asked to solve a problem defined by the teacher or suggested by themselves, using the techniques that have been demonstrated in the lessons.

Allow me to quote *Mindstorms* again:

One might ask why the teachers do not notice the difficulty children
have in learning BASIC. The answer is simple: Most teachers do not
expect high performance from most students, especially in a domain of
work that appears to be as 'mathematical' and 'formal' as programming.
Thus the culture's general perception of mathematics as 'inaccessible'
bolsters the maintenance of BASIC, which in turn confirms these
perceptions.

In Denmark we tend to use pocket calculators to crunch numbers in mathematics or to find the sine of an unfriendly angle, and save the computers for
more general problems such as sorting things out for people. We try to do this
in a manner that makes it clear that a machine is a tool in the hands of people,
and not the other way round!

7.4 APPLICATIONS OF COMAL

Shortly after we had implemented COMAL a great project started at the School
of Dentistry, University of Aarhus. They wanted to teach the dentists-to-be about
anatomy using Computer Aided Learning. They had already rejected BASIC as a
possible tool, and the only alternative they had was a very bad Algol compiler.
And I must say that we had a piece of good luck then. They tried COMAL and it
worked! The whole project became one of the most spectacular successes we
have ever seen in CAI in my country. As you may guess a lot of courseware has
been written in Denmark using COMAL since that event, and right now it is the
most used CAI language in Hamlet's fatherland. In this case the Danes were
not irresolute.

In 1978 some softwarehouses started to use COMAL to write programs for
business applications, and they must have been quite successful. It was only a
fortnight ago that I read an advertisement in a newspaper offering a job as
programmer in one of these houses. The main demand: Applicants should be
able to program in COMAL.

Latest news is that COMAL 80 is going to be used for process control. An
extended version running on CBM computers allows you to have assembly coded
subroutines called from COMAL as if they were normal user programmed
procedures. Since procedures may be used as functions in COMAL 80 a statement like this may very well appear in a Control COMAL program:

IF BIT(SMOKECONTROL,7) THEN EXEC SET(AIR'INTAKE,5)

With this facility the sky is the limit.

And now it is 8 years since the first sketches of COMAL were jotted down
on the back of a set of notes at the University of Aarhus. Since then we have
seen again and again that people reject BASIC as soon as they get a chance to

use COMAL. In the meantime BASIC has, however, spread like a plague in hundreds of versions some of which with such monstrous excrescences that they ought to be relegated to the theory of nightmares. The reason for this is quite clear. Since BASIC has not got procedures with parameters, new built-in functions have to be added to the interpreter all the time. Thus BASIC will go on growing more and more wild until one day it is finally strangled under the weight of its own deformed body.

The future belongs to languages of the Pascal family, because they are much more efficient tools than the Fortran/Cobol type of languages. Just take a look at Ada. In schools we must have a language of the same family to give our students a good start. But we cannot use unmodified professional languages. Not long ago I got a letter from an English computer scientist saying among other things, '...we teach Pascal to our students and we already agree with structured programming approach. However students who only take Computing as a minor subject in other diciplines find Pascal rather too much'. He is right. Pascal is rather too much for most of our students. But at the same time there is absolutely no doubt that BASIC is much too little.

We have tried to find an alternative in Denmark, COMAL is easy to learn and powerful to use. The students who want to get on to more professional high level languages find it natural to do so, and those who do not have such ambitions simply get their jobs done in a neat and clean way.

CHAPTER 8

Software standards in BASIC and COMAL

Roy Atherton, Bulmershe College of Higher Education

A brief review of some attempts at software standards in the 1970s is given and two areas in which progress is seen as a realistic possibility are suggested: the user-interface for computer assisted learning and program structure. The latter is discussed in some detail. Rules are given for writing well-structured programs in BASIC based on the notation of COMAL which may be used as a program design language. The problem of back-tracking through procedures is identified as a fairly common problem in CAL and other interactive programs and a solution is suggested.

> ...... That blessed mood
> In which the burden of the mystery,
> In which the heavy and the weary weight
> Of all this unintelligible world
> Is lightened. . . . . .
>
> *Michael,* William Wordsworth

8.1 PUBLISHED STANDARDS IN BASIC

There have been several attempts to produce standards for programs written in BASIC for educational purposes. Some examples are given:

(1) Guidelines for the Production of Software Packages for Education (NCC, 1974).
(2) Subset of BASIC for Education (MUSE C. 1975).
(3) MUSE Program Standards (MUSE, 1980).
(4) A Standard for CAL Dialogue (Advisory Unit for Computer Based Education, Hertfordshire, 1980).
(5) MUSE Database Standard (1980).

The NCC guidelines have been useful in enabling the Chelsea packages [1] to transfer easily to various machines but they have been largely ignored by schools because each enhancement of Kemeny and Kurtz's original BASIC (1966) has been regarded as a step forward by users. As BASIC has evolved year by year users have become less and less willing to settle for a minimal subset.

It was intended that the NCC guidelines should also help to facilitate the organisation of a software library for schools at NCC. This has not happened.

The attempt by MUSE in the mid seventies to produce an agreed subset (aimed essentially at DEC, Data General and other minicomputers) provoked endless discussion but eventually foundered partly because ways of handling strings and files were not in any sense reconcilable.

The MUSE standards of 1980 attempt to define *four* types of module which can be independent of the particular machine chosen or independent of the program in which the module may be embedded. Thus there are four possible types of module. There are, of course, difficulties with line numbers because a module may be written with a range of line numbers already used for another purpose in the main program. Thus there is a set of rules for numbering lines in a program. There are also reserved (two characters or two characters plus $) names for certain specified purposes, for example:

$ZX\$$ = string to be printed
ZX = X coord in characters
ZY = Y coord in characters
GX = number of X graphics units per character
GY = number of Y graphics units per character

It also recommended that all variable names should use two characters or two characters plus $ because this is the best that is possible in RML, PET, TANDY and APPLE computers.

The document contains 21 pages plus some standard subroutines. The section on standard commands for CAL dialogue gives a list which is different from the the Hertfordshire document on CAL. The MUSE standards again encounter the severe problems which arise from the nature of BASIC and the attempt to cater four four types of machine. It is fairly long for a technical document.

The Hertfordshire document on CAL is rather different. It gives advice about the design and writing of CAL packages. It emphasises the need to cater properly for users in a standard way and, though it has some 380Z examples, the paper grapples with the general problem of writing good CAL packages and does not attempt to establish more specific programming standards.

A much less ambitious document is the three-page MUSE Database standard which is a set of recommendations for files which may be used in school administration. Standardisation in this area may not be possible yet. The reason is simply that data structures and data processing have not yet been thoroughly analysed and worked out in the way that control structures have been. Certainly there are some good ideas which might well become standards but that is not the same thing. It can be argued that the definitions of record and file structures can be made independently of systems standards, but it does seem more sensible to pay attention to fundamental things first.

Another area of difficulty concerns what Bob Lewis calls 'critical mass'. It is suggested that a teacher, who always has a choice to use or not to use computer aids, is more likely to take a positive view of a package which has a number of related programs than he will of one odd item. Such a package would have emerged from a study of syllabuses and classroom practice because it would be difficult to put together a large realistic package in any other way. The advantages for the teacher are that there is a substantial benefit in quantity in return for his own effort in organising and familiarising himself with the material, as well as better integration with the usual pattern of work.

There seems no compelling reason why progress should not be made in the area of standards for the user interface and the Hertfordshire document is a serious attempt at guidelines for CAL dialogue. This and other similar documents could make a useful contribution and might reduce the number of occurrences of puzzlement or disenchantment amongst non-specialist computer users who are now a very substantial number indeed.

The question of programming and documentation standards is much more difficult. The 1970s witnessed a sort of competition amongst manufacturers of minicomputers to improve their BASIC systems. For example, the facilities for string handling in BASIC were not widespread and not uniformly good in 1970. Now they are more or less uniformly good in the sense that one can do what is necessary, but the notation is by no means uniform. There is still some variation in the quality of file-handling facilities and an enormous variation in type and quality of graphics.

A further major difficulty with BASIC is the reliance on line numbers as an inherent part of the program. While they are useful for editing and perhaps only a minor irritant within a single program, they become a major source of trouble when attempting to transfer procedures or subroutines to a program from another program or from a library of procedures. Anyone involved in non-trivial software writing or software transfer knows that one can change all the line numbers in a procedure to avoid clashing with line numbers already used, re-save the procedure, load the main program, merge the altered procedure with it, and finally delete the altered procedure from the disc. Having done all of this it is then necessary to ensure that there are no clashes between variables in the host program and those of the procedure.

COMAL [2] goes some way towards a solution with properly named, closed procedures, but it is still necessary to be careful about line numbers when merging two segments of a program. In these circumstances the writer takes the view that detailed programming standards for BASIC must be either accept-ably simple and inadequately detailed or comprehensive and unacceptably complex. There are still some major problems in language and operating system design to be solved before we arrive at a framework within which programming standards can succeed. However, there are some areas of possible standardisation which need attention and which are now sufficiently well understood for progress to be made on a basis which is not likely to change rapidly and in ways which are not lengthy and technical to describe. These are the user interface, already discussed, and program structure, discussed below.

8.2 ASSUMPTIONS ABOUT BASIC

Assumptions in this paper are available in a large number of BASIC implement-ations and they will be described briefly.

[   ] means that parts within are optional
a, b, c . . . . z are numeric variables
A, B, C are numeric expressions

FOR loop
SYNTAX

FOR X = A TO B STEP C
—
—
—
NEXT X

EXAMPLE

FOR p = 1 TO 4
PRINT "Dig a post hole"
NEXT p

CONDITIONAL statement
SYNTAX

IF ⟨condition⟩ THEN ⟨statement⟩

EXAMPLE

IF s = 1 THEN PRINT "Dig a half metre hole"

GOTO statement
SYNTAX

    GOTO ⟨line number⟩.

EXAMPLE

    GOTO 70

Multiple Branching
SYNTAX

    ON A GOTO ⟨line number⟩, ⟨line number⟩, ...

EXAMPLE

    ON INT(RND(0)*3)+1 GOTO 30,80,120

Notes: (1) INT(RND(0)*3)+1 is the equivalent of RND(1,3)
        (2) Depending on the value of the expression control will go to line 30,
        line 80 or line 120.

SYNTAX

    ON A GOSUB ⟨line number⟩, ⟨line number⟩, ...

Note: The effect is the same as ON . . . GOTO except that a subroutine jump
is performed. See the next item.

Subroutine
SYNTAX

    GOSUB ⟨line number⟩

⟨line number⟩ —
        —
        —
        —
        RETURN

EXAMPLE

    GOSUB 200

    200 PRINT "Subroutine"
    210 RETURN

Note: A BASIC subroutine is a primitive form of procedure. It is not properly
named and its start is not defined. Otherwise it performs like a simple
COMAL procedure without formal parameters.

Random Number Function

Most BASICs allow only the generation of a number in the range 0 to 1 by some function like RND(1). It is also a little unusual to find a numeric value acceptable as a condition so that one has to write:

IF s = 1 THEN PRINT "Ground is soft"

rather than

IF s THEN PRINT "Ground is soft"

This is no great loss because neither statement is particularly helpful to the reader. But it does mean that binary decisions are best treated on the lines:

s = RND(1)
IF s < 0.5 THEN . . . . . .

8.3 STRUCTURAL PRINCIPLES AND RULES

The central theme of structured programming is that structure should reflect function. This theme can be considered in three stages: problem analysis/program design, coding and presentation.

A structure diagram, achieved essentially by a process of top down analysis, or an equivalent (iterative graph or design structure diagram) might be the result of good program design. It is equally acceptable to think in COMAL and, in effect, write a COMAL program as the program design for conversion into BASIC. Each structural element of the program should have one entry point and one exit point. Elements should be related only in simple, correct ways: sequential, subordinate, procedure calls.

The coding should reflect the program design, that is, it should indicate what the program will actually do. The trouble here is that a running program is a dynamic thing whereas a program on paper is static. That is why it should show clearly which parts are loops and what type, and which parts are decisions. It should also show clearly the function of any procedures. Dijkstra puts all this very succinctly.

> We should do our utmost to shorten the conceptual gap between
> the static program and the dynamic process, to make the corres-
> pondence between the program (spread out in text space) and the
> process (spread out in time) as trivial as possible.

Obviously programs must be as easy as possible to read. If they are not readable they cannot reflect anything comprehensible by people.

The good presentation of a program in BASIC is often frustrated by the system. Keywords in upper case, spacing, indenting are all helpful, but most BASIC implementations remove some or all of these things even if the programmer puts them in. The only aid to good presentation in many systems is the REM statement. Nevertheless it is helpful to write programs in this way before they are keyed in to the machine. It is probably better to publish them in this way too though the risk of error is higher when machine-produced listings are not used. See [3] for many examples.

In deciding on the particular BASIC constructs the following rules have been observed.

(1)   The constructs will simulate very closely the structures of COMAL.

(2)   REM statements will be used where necessary to show explicitly the opening, closing and intermediate keywords of each construct.

(3)   The target of GOTO or GOSUB statements will always be a REM statement so that additions or deletions can take place within the structure without causing a GOTO or GOSUB to lose its target.

(4)   Indenting will be used and the distinction between keywords and other words of programs will be maintained though it is recognised that most systems would not recognise or would remove such features. For this purpose words of COMAL used in REM statements will be treated as keywords.

(5)   The following structures of COMAL and other languages have been shown in theory and in practice to be adequate for the vast majority of programming needs with only occasional use of the GOTO statement.

REPETITION   FOR .... NEXT (exit on counter)
                REPEAT .... UNTIL (exit on condition)
                WHILE .... ENDWHILE (exit on condition)

DECISION   IF ... THEN ... ELSE (binary)
                CASES   (multiple)

MODULARITY   PROCEDURES

Notes: (1) Decision is also called selection.
           (2) All the structures should be *global*. That is, any structure can fit inside any other. All have equal status.
           (3) In addition to the global structures there are three 'one-liners' used with a single statement, and no closing keyword. These are the FOR and WHILE repetition structures plus IF. . . THEN without ELSE.

8.4 ESSENTIAL STRUCTURES IN COMAL AND BASIC

The essential structures will be illustrated by means of a specially constructed problem which provides a simple, if somewhat artificial, context for discussion. The problem is to simulate what would happen if a workman was 'programmed' by his foreman with the following instructions:

"I want a corner post hole at each corner of this field and along each side

you must dig post holes fifteen metres apart. Where the ground is soft we
need a half-metre hole and elsewhere, a third metre hole. If there is a tree
in the way get Fred to deal with it. Tell him what size the tree is: small,
medium or large and he will know what to do. You can get the length of
each side of the field from a data sheet".

Fred's instructions for the process "treechop" are:

"For a small tree just pull it out. Cut a medium tree above the base and pull
out the root. A large tree will have to be cut down and its roots dug out."

Various parts of the solution will be treated separately to illustrate the
various structures.

8.4.1 FOR loop
COMAL

```
FOR post := 1 TO 4 DO
    PRINT "Dig a corner post"
NEXT post
```

BASIC

```
10 FOR p = 1 TO 4
20   PRINT "Dig a corner post"
30 NEXT p
```

8.4.2 REPEAT loop
COMAL

```
fieldlength := 100
REPEAT
  PRINT "Dig a hole"
  fieldlength := fieldlength − 15
UNTIL fieldlength < 15
```

BASIC

```
10 f = 100
20 REM REPEAT
30   PRINT "Dig a hole"
40   f = f − 15
50 IF f >= 15 THEN GOTO 20
```

Notes: (1) The condition has been reversed. Some programmers would write:

$$NOT(f < 15)$$

in order to preserve a strong relationship between analysis and coding.
(2) The end of the REPEAT loop is not as obvious as it might be, but it
might be, but it seems verbose to add an extra line REM UNTIL f < 15.

8.4.3 Binary Decision
COMAL

```
soft := RND(1)
IF soft < 0.5 THEN
    PRINT "Dig a half metre hole"
ELSE
    PRINT "Dig a third metre hole"
ENDIF
```

BASIC

```
10 s = RND(1)
20 IF s < 0.5 THEN GOTO 50
30   PRINT "Dig a half metre hole"
40 GOTO 70
50 REM ELSE
60   PRINT "Dig a third metre hole"
70 REM ENDIF
```

Notes: (1) Some BASIC allow local forms of IF. . . THEN . . . ELSE and in simple cases one could write:
IF s < 0.5 THEN PRINT "Dig a half metre hole" ELSE PRINT "Dig a third metre hole"
Such 'one liners' are better for the simple cases but students will need to simulate the global IF . . . THEN . . . ELSE structure at some stage.
(2) The rectangles are drawn at the end of a line because, at the time of writing, the line number target is not known. When it becomes known the rectangles are filled.

8.4.4 Multiple Decision
COMAL
The following program segment will only work if the string variable *treetype$* is given a value "small", "medium" or "large". This will be done in the next section.

```
CASE treetype$ OF
WHEN "small"
    PRINT "Pull out tree"
WHEN "medium"
    PRINT "Cut above base. Pull out root"
WHEN "large"
    PRINT "Cut down tree. Dig out root"
OTHERWISE
    PRINT "Tree type not known"
ENDCASE
```

BASIC

The ON. . . .GOSUB construct only works with numeric expressions so 0,1,2 will be used instead of different tree sizes given as words.

```
20 ON T GOSUB 40 , 70 , 100
30 GOTO 130
40 REM WHEN 0
50    PRINT "Pull out tree"
60 RETURN
70 REM WHEN 1
80    PRINT "Cut above base. Pull out root"
90 RETURN
100 REM WHEN 2
110    PRINT "Cut down tree. Dig out root"
120 RETURN
130 REM ENDCASE
```

8.4.5 Procedure

The procedure is illustrated by placing the treechop routine between the keywords which open and close a procedure. The variable *treetype$* becomes a formal parameter which is given a value by a simple mechanism in the main program. It is convenient at this stage to show the complete program in COMAL.

```
DIM treetype$ OF 6, treesize(3) OF 6
FOR k:= 1 TO 3 DO READ treesize$(k)
FOR side := 1 TO 4 DO
    PRINT "Dig a corner post hole"
    READ sidelength
    REPEAT
        tree := RND(0,1)
        IF tree THEN EXEC treechop(treesize$(RND(1,3)))
        soft := RND(0.1)
        IF soft THEN
            PRINT "Dig a half metre hole"
        ELSE
            PRINT "Dig a third metre hole"
        ENDIF
        sidelength := sidelength - 15
    UNTIL sidelength < 15
next side
PROC treechop(treetype$)
    CASE treetype$ OF
    WHEN "small"
        PRINT "Pull out tree"
```

```
WHEN "medium"
    PRINT "Cut above base. Pull out root"
WHEN "large"
    PRINT "Cut down tree. Dig out root"
OTHERWISE
    PRINT "Tree type not known"
ENDCASE
ENDPROC treechop
DATA "small", "medium", "large"
DATA 100,120,140,110
```

BASIC
The program can be constructed in BASIC according to the rules given. The subroutine call and definition take the forms shown, the parameter value, ts, being fixed before the call.

```
60 ts = INT(RND(1)*3)
70 IF t ⟨ 0.5 THEN GOSUB  200
   —
   —
   —
   —

200 REM TREECHOP
   —
   —
   —
   —

280 RETURN
```

The complete program in BASIC is not given for reasons of space.

8.4.6 WHILE loop
The need for the WHILE loop can be appreciated by considering an exceptional case of a field with a wedge shape so that one side is, say, 12 m long. In this case the program would give an incorrect result because it would place a post between two corner posts only 12 m apart. In general one should be able to exit from a loop after zero executions of its content.

This can be achieved by deleting the two lines:

```
REPEAT
```
and UNTIL sidelength ⟨ 15
and replacing them with:
```
    WHILE sidelength ⟩= 15 DO
    ENDWHILE
```

The condition is tested at the start of the loop and if it is not true exit takes place immediately.

The BASIC equivalent is:

```
50 REM WHILE
60 IF 1 < 15 THEN GOTO  160
    _
    _
    _

150 GOTO   50
160 REM ENDWHILE
```

8.4.7 Complex Structures

The structure of the post-holes problem is not a difficult one to handle. Not all problems can be solved in a straightforward manner even if the language provides all the possible help. An example of an inherently awkward structure and how it may be treated in COMAL is given in the next section.

8.5 A STRUCTURAL PROBLEM IN CAL PROGRAMS

User Requirements

A number of computer assisted learning programs are based on the following criteria:

(1) The system should not accept wrong responses. These are either ignored or a message is given with a further opportunity.

(2) It should be almost impossible to 'break' the system.

(3) A user, however wayward or timid, should be patiently guided towards ultimate success.

(4) The 'game' should be capable of being used easily by an inexperienced non-specialist of any intelligence, including, for example, average ability six-year-olds.

(5) The teacher should have flexible control of the system. By means of 'secret' codes he should be able to access parts of the program which change values or create new files of data.

The above criteria and the interactive nature of such programs tends to make them convoluted. They can be written in BASIC and they are usually extremely hard to read. They are not easy to write in COMAL but control (readability) can be retained and difficulties can be minimised by using procedures and setting flags to determine how much 'back-tracking' is done in different circumstances. An example will clarify the problem and a possible solution.

Spelling Game

After setting up arrays of words and initializing the game it proceeds essentially as follows:

(1) The child types a one, two or three digit number terminated by a dot.

(2) The child then attempts to spell the word corresponding to the picture on the card with that number. Since incorrect letters are ignored the only possible outcome is a correct spelling of the word. If all else fails this can be achieved by penning a finger along the letter keys.

(3) When the word has been spelled some response such as "Good" or a few asterisks signals that the machine is ready to receive a new number in preparation for a new word.

The first complication is that, at stage (1), there are a few possible acceptable characters instead of just a first digit so the outline scheme is roughly as follows:

A boxed rectangle indicates a procedure definition.
The secret code for access to the files routines is "*".

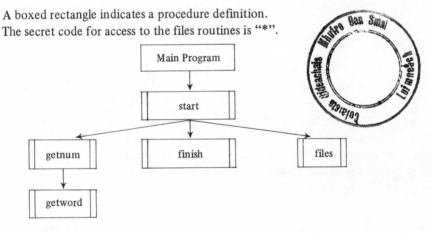

(1) During a game control normally passes repeatedly through the sequence *start, getnum, getword.*

(2) If *finish* or *files* are used then control must pass back through *start* to the main program for a new game to be set going.

Program Structure

```
REPEAT
   EXEC initialise
   REPEAT
      EXEC start
   UNTIL flag2$ = "INT"
UNTIL 2 = 1
```

```
PROC start
  REPEAT
    GET char$
    IF char$="*" THEN EXEC files
    IF char$="F" THEN EXEC finish
    IF digit THEN EXEC getnum
  UNTIL flag$ = "START"
ENDPROC

PROC getnum
  −
  −
  −
  EXEC getword
ENDPROC

PROC getword
  −
  −
  −
  flag$:="START"
ENDPROC
```

This will ensure that when one word has been spelt control returns through the procedures to the inner loop of the main program. EXEC start will then enable a new word to be spelt. This sequence continues until "F" is typed typed causing the procedure *finish* to be entered.

```
PROC finish
  −
  −
  −
  flag$:="START"
  flag2$:="INIT"
ENDPROC
```

The additional setting of flag2$ to "INIT" causes re-entry to the outer loop of the main program for re-initialising the new game. The return from procedure *files* can be arranged in the same way because the object, re-initialisation for a new game, is the same.

This example is adapted from an actual program [4] originally written in BASIC with 31 GOTO statements. The COMAL version has none. There are some complications but they can be handled without serious difficulty because the structure is reasonably clear.

The difficulties in this type of programming arise from the specified requirements of the game. There is no very easy way to satisfy them.

One could, of course, try to use some GOTO statements but the whole approach would have to change. In many cases one could not use procedures to provide complete modularity because one cannot jump in and out of them.

Extension of Technique

A significant extension to the general problem arises if one wishes to move across from one procedure to another as shown.

This can be achieved by extending the condition for calling this procedure:

IF char$ = "F" OR flag3$ = "files" THEN EXEC files

Of course flag3$ must be set to "files" in the procedure where the decision is made. This is in addition to any requirements for taking control back up the structure. It should be added that one would not wish to make such a move in the program discussed but such requirements can arise.

8.6 CONCLUSIONS AND SUGGESTIONS

(1) The pressures against standardisation should not be underestimated. Individual and groups as well as companies inevitably will try to improve on anything or do things differently for other reasons.

(2) Standards can be achieved but they must be good standards. They must command the support of a substantial majority of well-informed people in the field. They must be realistic and acceptable to most users whether well-informed or not.

(3) Individuals can establish standards as well as committees. Algol 68 came from a committee but Pascal came, essentially, from an individual.

(4) If a committee is established it should be both expert and realistic. In an educational context this means that its members should be both technically competent and have experience and understanding of the relevant educational sector.

(5) There is great benefit to be gained from judicious standardisation but misguided standards are an abomination. Not only do they fail to propagate the best practices but they alienate precisely those people who might contribute most.

(6) The time seems right for establishing a European committee to guide the development of COMAL or some structured BASIC which is at least as good.

(7) Standards or guidelines for the way in which a system interacts with users would also seem appropriate and beneficial now.

(8) Standards in the fields of data structures and data processing, graphics, CAL programming and documentation are much more difficult. There is perhaps a need for discussion papers, more reflection, and perhaps more experience before more positive moves are made.

REFERENCES

[1] Lewis, R., *Compters in the Curriculum,* Schools Council Project, Edward Arnold, 1980.

[2] Christensen, B. R., *et al., COMAL 80 Programming Language,* (Nucleus Definition, March 1980), Available from Roy Atherton, Bulmershe College, Reading, UK.

[3] Atherton, R., *Structured Programming with COMAL 80,* Ellis Horwood, 1982.

[4] Atherton, R., *SPELL Documentation for a spelling game in ID COMAL,* Bulmershe College, Reading, UK 1980.

CHAPTER 9

PETCAI: A system for development and delivery of computer-assisted instruction

Danny Doyle, Gawcott, Bucks.

This presentation is about a new product, which has been developed for the PET personal computer, called PETCAI. PETCAI is a program that enables teachers in education and professional trainers in industry to prepare automated courses of instruction. It also provides a general system for information retrieval applications such as filing teletext and viewdata pages. However, before going on to look at PETCAI in detail, I'd like to spend a little time reviewing some of the major historical factors that have contributed to the development of Computer-Assisted Instruction (CAI) as a method of teaching.

9.1 A HISTORY OF COMPUTER ASSISTED INSTRUCTION

Influence of the early Greeks on instruction and approaches to teaching

The primary objective of CAI is to provide individualised instruction − one learner and one teacher. Of course this is not a new method of teaching, the system of having one teacher and one pupil can be traced back to early Greek time. In those days, for example, the youth of Athens were taught by the most learned men of the day. Socrates was probably the most famous exponent of this type of instruction, and many of the techniques he employed are to be found in modern-day CAI. Socrates believed that all ideas are given to a person at birth, and that his task was to help the student become aware of these innate ideas. Because he saw himself in the role of a midwife, giving birth to ideas, his method of teaching is sometimes called the **'Maieutic' method**: 'Maieutikos' in Greek means 'midwifery'!

The Socratic approach to teaching

In the Socratic approach to teaching a small unit of information is presented, followed by a question. Now it is obvious that by asking a question the teacher can determine whether or not the student has comprehended the material he has just received. But the question serves another important purpose, it encourages a dialogue between the student and the teacher, and thus maintaining the student in a non-passive role during the lesson. Similarly, the CAI author tries to structure his lessons so that they are conversational, and does this by using the basic formula of Socrates: a statement, a question, then a reply to provide feedback to the student. In this way the student benefits by remaining active in the learning situation, and progressing at a rate that is directly related to his own performance and comprehension.

The Aristotelian approach to teaching
One of Socrates students was Plato, who in turn taught Aristotle. Although little is known about the techniques used by Aristotle in teaching, it is widely believed that he relied mainly on the lecture method. His students would take notes of what he had said, in the same way that students take notes from their lecturers today. This method of Aristotle was in complete contrast to that of Socrates, or Plato, and there were other things in which he differed from his predecessors. In particular, he did not accept Socrates' belief that all ideas are innate.

Importance of association in learning
Aristotle assumed that all knowledge was gained through experience, and based on this assumption, he put forward an idea that is of practical interest to CAI authors today. The idea was that learning and memory are based on experience and association. We use association, for example, to teach new terminology – a new word is presented along with its definition. Later, if association has taken place, we can trigger recall of the word definition by presenting just the word by itself. As well as new terminology and vocabulary, CAI authors also use association to introduce students to new ideas and concepts. The CAI author should always be careful, when using association, that new words, or ideas, are always defined in terms that are already known to the student. If not, students may well end up by being able to 'parrot' back strings of words without any real understanding of their meaning.

First steps towards automated instruction
We have now seen that methods and ideas introduced over two thousand years ago have an immediate and practical relevance to today's CAI author and teacher. Obviously though, the early Greek teachers could not have envisaged the prospect of instruction being automated. The first step towards automated instruction was taken in the 1920s. Working at Ohio State University in America, an educational psychologist, called Sidney L. Pressey, invented a device that could be used for self-administered, self-scoring tests.

Since testing itself is a form of teaching, Pressey reasoned that a machine could be built to take over some routine teacher functions. As an outcome of this idea, Pressey wrote a paper, published in 1927 called, *A machine for the*

Automatic Teaching of Drill Material. The paper described a machine that could display a menu of answers, and which had a mechanism for a student to indicate his selection. The machine could provide feedback on whether the student's answer was correct or not.

Pressey's contribution to CAI development is notable because, as well as describing his machines in terms of labour-saving devices, he also discussed how the machines could be used to implement the principles of learning and instruction. In the same way the CAI author has a similar task of trying to implement known principles when developing instructional material.

Introduction of programmed instruction

Although Pressey continued work in this field, little progress was made in the automation of instruction until the 1950s. It was Professor B. F. Skinner, working at Harvard University, who gave a new impetus to the development of CAI technology by pioneering a system of teaching called, **Programmed Instruction.** Using the basic idea of Pressey, Skinner invented a mechanical teaching machine, and developed a method of automated teaching, which obliged the student to 'construct' his own response to a question (rather than choosing from a menu of replies as with the Pressey method).

Skinner's approach to teaching placed considerable emphasis on the need for positive reinforcement, and his lesson material was organised to minimize the possibility of the student giving an incorrect response, and so maximised the amount of positive reinforcement received by the student. This strategy maintained a high level of motivation. However, Skinner's programmed lessons were 'linear', or 'non-branching', each student received the same sequence of instructional units as every other student. There were other researchers who felt that the possibility of student error should not be excluded from the learning process, and that an automated system of instruction should take into account the differences between ability and proclivity. What was needed, it was argued, was a system that combined the features of Programmed Instruction with the capability to dynamically modify the instruction in step with the changing needs of the student.

Non-linear programming

At about the same time as Skinner was developing Programmed Instruction, another researcher, called Norman A. Crowder, was working on a technique of **Intrinsic Programming.** Intrinsic Programming is also called 'non-linear' to differentiate it from Skinner's 'linear' programming. Using the Intrinisic Programming technique, the student's response determines the next step in one of several paths through the instructional material.

This differs fundamentally from Skinner's method, where there is no deviation from the 'prime path' of correct answers. The foregoing comparison of Skinner and Crowder reflects a difference of opinion over method, but the

CAI author should not regard the techniques of 'linear' and 'non-linear' as conflicting alternatives. Both techniques can be used successfully in Computer-Assisted Instruction, and the CAI author should apply whichever one he feels is best suited to the subject matter at hand.

Comparative studies in CAI and conventional instruction
Since the 1950s the research has continued. The comparisons in CAI research studies show significant benefits of CAI learning as compared with conventional instruction techniques. Students learn faster and achieve higher test scores when using CAI than they do with conventional instruction. This is not to say that Computer-Assisted Instruction is the answer to all of today's educational problems, or that the computer should become a surrogate teacher. But, as has been found already in science, industry and commerce, the application of computers derives maximum benefit when the machine is used to complement, rather than substitute, human activity. In particular, the computer has already demonstrated its effectiveness as a teaching aid in universities, industry, and the military to present drill and practice as well as tutorial material.

The need for other tools
One of the problems encountered in the application of CAI has not been in the technology, but in the writing of subject material. On the large mainframe computers the availability of sophisticated 'Author Languages' has largely resolved the problem of lesson development.

The author languages provide an interface to the computer, which allows the subject matter expert and curriculum specialist to develop CAI teaching material, without the need to become a computer specialist. However, until now there has been little progress in providing similar tools for the personal computer user — which is why this is a good time to take a look at PETCAI!

9.2 A FRAME SYSTEM FOR THE MICROCOMPUTER: PETCAI

What is PETCAI?
PETCAI is a system that enables training specialists, and teachers to prepare automated courses of instruction. Although primarily designed for use in the field of education, PETCAI can be used for many information retrieval applications. This is particularly true in the case where information can be structured around a menu-driven scheme. A good example of this type of information structure is to be found in the textual display systems for television, which are being broadcast by the BBC and commercial television companies.

Modes of operation
The system supports two basic modes of operation

    (1) AUTHOR mode — development of course material
    (2) STUDENT mode — delivery of course material.

Instructional material prepared for use under PETCAI is hierarchical in structure. The basic unit is called a **FRAME**. A number of FRAMEs constitute a **LESSON**. A number of LESSONs constitute a course as shown below:

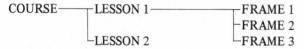

Each lesson is identified by assigning it a label of up to ten characters in length. FRAMEs within a lesson are given a unique three digit identifier. A FRAME consists of two parts which are called **PAGES**. These pages are referred to as the **TEXT** page, and the **CONTROL** page. Fig. 9.1 shows a sample layout of the TEXT and CONTROL pages.

Subject: Astronomy   Frame: 017

As you know the universe is made up from many different elements. See if you can tell me the two most common elements found in the composition of a star.

Type in the names separated by a single space, then press RETURN.

ANTICIPATED RESPONSE	FRAME	PNTS
1) HYDROGEN HELIUM	, NXT,	+1
2) HELIUM HYDROGEN	, 018,	+1
3) HYDROGEN	, 019,	+0
4) HELIUM	, 020,	+0
5)	, ,	
6)	, ,	
7)	, ,	
8)	, ,	

IF THE NUMBER OF RETRIES EXCEEDS	002
THEN WE WILL CONTINUE WITH FRAME	010
FOR A BAD REPLY, OR 'RETURN' GO TO	099
IF NO RESPONSE IS RECEIVED WITHIN	120
SECONDS THE NEXT FRAME WILL BE	098
PHONETIC MODE HAS BEEN SWITCHED OFF	

Fig. 9.1 – Text page (top) and control page (bottom) of a frame.

Author mode

When PETCAI is placed into execution, the system asks the user to indicate in which of the two basic modes of operation he wishes to work. If **AUTHOR** mode is selected, the system solicits a subject title, which is used to identify and label all subsequently referenced FRAMEs during the development session. The main task of preparing the instructional FRAMEs is accomplished through use of the PETCAI text editor. The PETCAI text editor is an extended version of the PET screen editor, which provides additional functions such as: repeat on all keys, line insert, line delete, and a modified clear-screen command. The editor also provides a set of directives for the manipulation of FRAMEs between the floppy disk and the PET. When using the editor to prepare FRAMEs, the author is limited to a screen area bounded by the top and bottom lines. This effectively inhibits the normal scrolling of text, which would be undesirable when editing FRAME displays. The bottom and top lines of the screen are reserved areas, and the author is prevented from entering text into either line. The top line is used to display the subject title and FRAME index. The bottom line is reserved for **STUDENT** mode, and is used as input area for student responses. An editor command is provided to enable the author to conveniently switch between the TEXT page and the CONTROL page of a FRAME.

Because both the TEXT page and the CONTROL page are maintained in memory, the switching of pages appears to be almost instantaneous. Fig. 9.2 shows how the CONTROL page appears when it is first displayed. The CONTROL page represents a form with blank areas which are completed by the author. The CONTROL page display is protected, the author is only permitted to enter text, or values, into predefined 'fields'. Moving between fields is very simple. Using the RETURN, or cursor-control keys on the PET keyboard, the author can, depending on which he depresses, position the cursor to the start of the next or previous field. The top half of the CONTROL page contains a set of fields numbered 1 through 8. Each of these fields contains 3 subfields, which are labelled: **ANTICIPATED RESPONSE**, 'FRAME', and **PNTS**. The subfield labelled, 'ANTICIPATED RESPONSE', is used by the author to enter a string of characters that will be matched with the student's response. If a match occurs then the next FRAME to be displayed will be the one whose index is coded in the 'FRAME' subfield. A value in the range, -9 to $+99$, can be entered in the 'PNTS' subfield. This value will be added to a score counter whenever a match is made between the student's reply and the anticipated response. The bottom half of the CONTROL page is mainly concerned with specifying limits and handling contingencies.

ANTICIPATED RESPONSE	FRAME	PNTS
1)	, ,	
2)	, ,	
3)	, ,	
4)	, ,	
5)	, ,	
6)	, ,	
7)	, ,	
8)	, ,	
IF THE NUMBER OF RETRIES EXCEEDS	999	
THEN WE WILL CONTINUE WITH FRAME	NXT	
FOR A BAD REPLY, OR 'RETURN' GO TO	NXT	
IF NO RESPONSE IS RECEIVED WITHIN	999	
SECONDS THE NEXT FRAME WILL BE	NXT	
PHONETIC MODE HAS BEEN SWITCHED OFF		

Fig. 9.2 – Initial status of control page.

There are two types of limitation that can be imposed on the student during a lesson session: the number of attempts made by the student to answer a question can be limited by coding a suitable value in the **RETRIES** field. Likewise, a time limit can be set on the time taken by the student to respond by coding a value, specified in seconds, in the **RESPONSE** field. (As a general rule the author should avoid imposing time limits on a student: a principle of CAI is that the student should be allowed to progress at his own rate.) If either of the limits described are exceeded, then the author can program a branch to another part of the lesson by specifying the appropriate FRAME indices in the relevant part of the CONTROL page. Similarly, the **BAD REPLY** field allows the author to cater for the situation where a student inputs an unexpected reply. Of course an unexpected reply may be due to a word being mistyped by the student. PETCAI incorporates a feature to allow for spelling mistakes. The author has the option to enable or disable the feature by coding an **ON** or **OFF** directive in the **PHONETIC MODE** field. If the feature is turned on, then a student reply that fails to match with any of the anticipated responses coded in the CONTROL page, will be converted to a phonetic equivalent and be re-matched with a phonetic equivalent of the anticipated responses.

Phonetic — spelling algorithm
The algorithm used for the word conversion is based on the following scheme:

(1) Each letter in the original word is converted thus:

Original	Converted
a, e, i, o, u, y	a
h, w	h
l	l
b, p, f, v	b
m, n	m
d, t	d
c, g, j, k, q, s, x, z	c
r	r

(2) All h's are removed unless h is the first letter.
(3) Multiple characters are removed.
(4) All vowels are removed.

The algorithm, though simple, is surprisingly effective, except for words containing silent consonants.

Having described how the CONTROL and TEXT pages of a FRAME are used, it can be seen that building a **LESSON** consists of cycling through a sequence of entering lesson text and questions into the TEXT frame, filling in the CONTROL page 'form', and then commanding the system to write the FRAME to disk.

Student mode

We will now go on to look at the **STUDENT** mode of operation. When the student is asked by the system to identify himself, and state the subject he wishes to study. PECTAI then checks to see if the student is resuming study of a previously suspended session. It is possible at any point during the lesson to terminate the session, in which case a student record is created on disk with the necessary information to restart the lesson at the point where the student left off. If the student is not resuming a previous session, then the system automatically selects the TEXT page of the first FRAME. Once into the lesson, PETCAI will use the student's input, combined with the coded information in the CONTROL pages, to monitor and adjust the student's path through the lesson material. Note that all text displayed during the student session is protected from inadvertant erasure by disabling certain parts of the PET keyboard, and only allowing the replies to be input on the bottom line of the screen.

The PETCAI calculator

There is one other feature of PETCAI that is available in both STUDENT and AUTHOR modes which should be mentioned. A powerful calculator facility can be invoked by entering the @CALC command. When the calculator is called the current contents of the screen is saved and replaced with the **CALCULATOR** page.

Within the CALCULATOR page the user can name and assign values to any one of the ten displayed registers. Using BASIC style algebraic notation, functional relationships can be declared between the registers. A powerful recalculation feature allows a single register value to be altered so that all dependent registers are simultaneously updated. Fig. 9.3 shows a typical CALCULATOR page. When the user exits from the CALCULATOR, before restoring the previously saved screen display, the system saves the CALCULATOR display and all register contents for later use if required.

Hardware requirements

That concludes the description of the software features available under PETCAI. Before finishing the presentation, just a few words on the hardware needed to run PECTAI. The minimum configuration required is a 32K PET using the BASIC 4.0 ROMS and a floppy disk drive (the level of DOS is not critical). A printer is not essential, but is desirable.

```
┌─────────────────────────────────────────────────────────┐
│                 PETCAI  CALCULATOR  PAGE                  │
│                                                           │
│   SPEED                         100                       │
│   TIME                          10                        │
│   DISTANCE=SPEED*TIME           1000                      │
│   LENGTH                        30.23                     │
│   WIDTH                         10                        │
│   AREA=LENGTH*WIDTH             302.3                     │
│   REG 7                         0                         │
│   REG 8                         0                         │
│   REG 9                         0                         │
│   REG 10                        0                         │
│   ?                                                       │
│                                                           │
└─────────────────────────────────────────────────────────┘
```

Fig. 9.3 – Example of a calculator page.

CHAPTER 10

Some techniques and applications of computer graphics in CAL

Adrian Oldknow, West Sussex Institute of Higher Education.

10.1 THE ROLE OF THE MICROCOMPUTER IN GRAPHICS

As is often the case with a change in technology there has been a period during which the classroom microcomputer has largely just been seen as a cheaper, more reliable and accessible replacement for an existing system such as a teletype linked by phone to a central computer. Thus much early effort was made to convert existing CAL packages originally designed to run on computers supporting terminals for microcomputer use. However the classroom micro is capable of performing many functions that were inconceivable in the days of the teletype. For example digital input/output ports are standard on many micros and there are now many ingenious examples of their application in science laboratories and in control work in craft, design and technology projects. The facility offered by the classroom micro, using a TV or monitor as its output device, which most interests me is the ability to create, manipulate and store pictures.

However there was initially a hardware limitation on this ability. If you look closely at a character on the screen of, say, a PET you can see that it is made up by the illumination of a number of individual dots. Thus each character that the computer can display is represented by a pattern of dots in, say, an 8 × 8 array (or matrix) of dots — remembering that for letters and some other characters there will have to be blank rows and columns to separate them. This collection of dot-patterns is known as the **character set** of the computer and is produced by a special chip known as the **character generator**. It is thus possible to design one's own character set including, say, the Greek alphabet and to have a chip **blown** to one's own specification to generate it. Within the machine the code for each character is stored in a single byte (8 bits) of RAM — thus there are $2^8 = 256$ different characters that the machine can represent. Typically some of these will be reserved for 'special' characters, such as RETURN or 'clear the screen' or STOP; then there are the usual capital letters and numerals, together with all the other familiar symbols on the keyboard. Thereafter the manufacturer decided whether to provide upper and lower case letters, reverse fields etc. and how to use the remaining unused character code for 'picture-drawing elements' (graphic symbols). Some manufacturers decided to follow the ASCII (American Standard Code for Information Interchange) character set using upper and lower case letters and to use the teletext system for graphic symbols (such as can be seen on Ceefax, Oracle or Prestel) which consist of combinations of six small squares forming a 2×3 rectangle. Commodore implemented reverse field on all characters and provided two alternative character sets: one with a wide range of graphic symbols and the other with lower case letters and a reduced set of graphic symbols. To store the contents of the display screen containing, say, 25 lines with 40 characters per line requires just 1000 bytes (or 1K) of screen memory. However to be able to illuminate each individual dot independently would require $8 \times 8 \times 1000 = 64000$ bits $= 8000$ bytes, which was more than the total available user memory (RAM) on the early versions of the PET.

Thus designing pictures involved laying out a design on graph paper and then seeing how best to approximate it from the graphic symbols implemented on a particular machine. This skill was rather like that required for producing mosaics or stained glass. The problem of transfer of programs between different microcomputers was made even more difficult when pictures were involved. I managed to do this for the JANE program written by the ITMA team in Plymouth for the teletext graphics of the Research Machine 380Z and produced a version that displays pictures on a PET. However, as the prices of memory chips have fallen dramatically over the past couple of years it is now possible to 'get at the dots' on nearly all the current microcomputers found in schools today — although in some cases this requires the installation of a special printed circuit board for the so-called 'high resolution graphics' (or h.r.g.). I have suggested a layout of 320×200 dots requiring 8K of RAM for monochrome display as typical, but, of course, there is wide variations between manufacturers. The term used for the dot (actually a small rectangle) used as the basic picture-making element is the **pixel**. For a monochrome display only 1 bit per pixel is required, but with 2 bits per pixel you can have $2^2 = 4$ colours, 3 bits gives 8 colours and 4 bits yields 16 colours. The colours can be represented as shades of grey from black to white for a monochrome TV or monitor or can be displayed on a colour television or monitor. Unfortunately colour televisions are expensive enough and do not always give very good reproduction and colour monitors are very expensive indeed, so although colour graphics are a practicable proposition they will be much more so as modern developments in display technology work their way through to the market place.

As all the machines I have met that have high resolution graphics have standard instructions with BASIC to plot a point at a given position and to draw a line segment from the last point reached to a given position it is now a practicable proposition to write picture drawing programs which though not entirely device-independent can easily be changed to run on different machines. In this article I shall describe some of the techniques I have found useful and some of the applications to which they have been put. A very useful feature that some machines implement is the ability to plot a text string at a particular location on the graphics screen, so that diagrams can be labelled or text and drawings can be interspersed. Another is the idea of an 'area-primitive' — that is, an instruction to fill in a particular shape with a given colour or shade. Until recently those machines that did offer this facility used rectangles with edges parallel to the display screen specified by the co-ordinates of, say, the lower left and upper right corners, but some newer arrivals are using triangles in general position as their basic area-filling units and these are much more versatile. However for the purpose of this article I shall concentrate on line drawing techniques because of their widespread applicability.

Many of the computer graphics techniques that have been developed over the past thirty years were designed for use on large computer installations driving high quality 'refresh-tube' graphics terminals (which work like an oscilloscope by controlling a single electron beam by deflection coils), hard copy devices such as flat-bed and drum plotters and input devices such as digitisers, tablets and light pens. The extremely high cost of this equipment limited the application of computer aided design (CAD) to a few very large industries (mainly ship, car and plane building) and consequently the literature on these techniques has remained quite specialised. Furthermore most of the techniques were implemented either in a compiled high level language such as Fortran or in assembler, whereas BASIC is still the common language of classroom micros. Thus the sample programs are written in BASIC but will, on the whole, run far more quickly if implemented in other languages.

10.2 TECHNIQUES FOR LINES, CIRCLES, CURVES AND SOLIDS

Lines

As all of the micros I have used for graphics have an instruction to draw an approximation to a line segment I shall just make reference to the most commonly used algorithms namely the DDA [1] (digital differential analyzer) and that due to Bresenham [2]. In each case the starting point of the line is taken as origin and the 'line' is composed of neighbouring pixels where each is a 'King's move' away from its predecessor. In fact each line is drawn as a combination of only 2 of the possible 8 moves — one horizontal or vertical (like a rook), the other diagonal (like a bishop) — depending upon which part of the plane the line lies within (see Fig. 10.1). Whichever technique is used to decide upon the combinations of rook's and bishop's moves some lines will always look 'lumpy'. Consider joining (0,0) to (100,3) — this will use 97 horizontal (easterly) and 3 diagonal (north-easterly) moves — so however the 3 diagonals are distributed within the 100 moves the line is bound to look jagged.

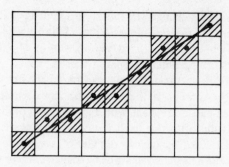

Fig. 10.1 – A set of pixels produced by Bresenham's algorithm joining (0, 0) to (8, 5).

Circles

As we have the ability to drawn line segments it is easy to construct polygons and so the general process for drawing curves consists of finding a suitable polygonal approximation. Consider drawing a circle of largish radius centered on the middle of the display screen. It is easiest to work as if the centre of the circle was the origin and subsequently to add, say, 160 to x-coordinates and 100 to y-coordinates before displaying them. This idea arises frequently and it is useful to have the distinction between an 'object space' system of co-ordinates for the body in question and an 'image space' system for the display screen. If we rearranged the cartesian equation of a circle $X^2 + Y^2 = R^2$ to determine Y values for given X values we have $Y = \pm \sqrt{R^2 - X^2}$ for $-R \leqslant X \leqslant R$. A possible BASIC program to draw a circle would be:

PROGRAM 1

```
100   R = 75 : R2 = R * R
110   FOR X = − R TO R
120   Y = SQR(R2 − X * X)
130   PLOT X + 160, 100 + Y
140   PLOT X + 160, 100 − Y
150   NEXT X
```

This produces many undesirable effects: it has lots of holes in it and it is far from symmetric.

An improvement is made on both counts if we use the parametric form $X = R\cos A$, $Y = R\sin A$ and decide on some suitable step size DA for incrementing the angle A — this is done by choosing the number of sides N of the approximating polygon and setting $A = 2\pi/N$ radians. If your machine does not have a value of π as a constant and if you find it difficult to remember π to 10 places then a useful trick is take π as 4 * ATN(1.0) since tan45° = 1 and 45° = $\pi/4$ radians.

PROGRAM 2

```
100  R = 75: N = 40: DA = 8 * ATN(1)/N
120  PLOT R + 160, 100
130  FOR A = DA TO 6.3 STEP DA
140  X = R * COS(A)
150  Y = R * SIN(A)
160  LINE X + 160, Y + 100
170  NEXT A
```

Note here that as the circle is approximated by line segments, and lines are drawn from the previous 'pen' position, it is essential to start the process by plotting the first point. This procedure should produce a symmetric image but on some machines it will appear to be slightly flattened and appear more like an ellipse than a circle. The reason for this is simple: the pixel may not be a square. Consider a 20 inch TV screen − the 20 inches is the diagonal measurement and the screen is a curved rectangle *not* a square. Different tubes can have different 'aspect ratios' but many are about 3:4 so our notional screen might have height 12 inches and width 16 inches. If the screen was divided uniformly into 200×320 pixels each would have height $12/200 = 0.06$ in. and width $16/320 = 0.05$ in. Thus each pixel would be a rectangle whose height was 20% more than its width. This can easily be cured by either introducing a 'squash factor' of $5/6$ by which y-coordinates are multiplied (in object space) or a 'stretch factor' of $6/5$ by which x-coordinates are multiplied. The other snag in Program 2 is that a sine and cosine have to be evaluated at each pass of the loop and this is quite costly in time.

A considerable improvement is obtained by dividing the circumference of the circle at equal intervals. If the neighbouring pair of points (x_n, y_n) and (x_{n+1}, y_{n+1}) subtend an angle D at the centre of the circle then their coordinates are related as follows:

$$x_{n+1} = x_n \cos D - y_n \sin D$$
$$y_{n+1} = x_n \sin D + y_n \cos D$$

where $\sin D$ and $\cos D$ have only to be evaluated once and then stay constant. The relations can be derived by a neat application of the matrix for a rotation through angle A. This yields the improved procedure:

PROGRAM 3

```
100  H = 160: K = 100: R = 75: N = 40
110  A = 8 * ATN(1)/N: XS = 1.2
120  X = R: Y = 0: S = SIN(A): C = COS(A)
130  PLOT X * XS + H, K
140  FOR I = 1 TO N
150  XT = X * C − Y * S
```

```
160   Y = X * S + Y * C
170   X = XT
180   LINE X * XS + H, Y + K
190   NEXT I
```

Not only does this procedure produce circles but, by changing the value of XS, also ellipses with axes parallel to the sides of the screen. To produce an ellipse in general position it is only necessary to apply a further rotation to the object coordinates generated within the loop (Fig. 10.2). Other methods are available for integer arithmetic or for point plotting (for example, Pitteway [3] and Gossling [4]) but the above procedure is very versatile.

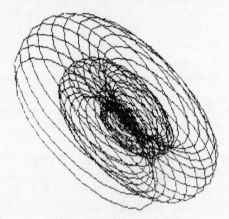

Fig. 10.2 – A family of ellipses.

Curves

As shown in the circle example the Cartesian equation of a curve is often awkward to work with and, on the whole, it is much easier to draw a curve from its parametric equations. Thus curves like cycloids, astroids, cardiods etc. are all very easy to generate (see Fig. 10.3) and here Lockwood [5] is an admirable source book. However many curves encountered in graphics, for example, the outline of a car, have no obvious mathematical identity and so the standard technique for representing such objects is to take a number of sample points on the profile and to fit a smooth curve passing through these points. These are many references to standard techniques for this process of 'interpolation' or 'curve-fitting' in the literature — particularly in books on numerical analysis. However, more recently, a technique has been developed which emulates the methods employed by 'loftsmen' in the shipbuilding and aircraft industries for 'fairing-out' smooth curves through given points. This consisted of bending a very springy wire (called a 'spline') to pass through holes in heavy flat weights (called 'ducks') which could be slid along the wire and placed over the given points. The curve formed by the springy wire pressing against its supports gives a smooth approximation to the desired profile. The mathematical analogy to this is the interpolating cubic spline which consists of a set of neighbouring cubic arcs which meet 'smoothly' at their joins. The fitting of such a spline requires the solution of a tri-diagonal set of linear equations and the details can be found in Greville [6].

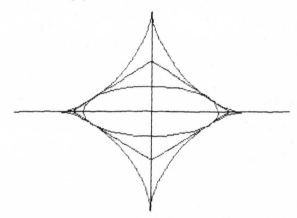

Fig. 10.3 – An astroid tangent to an ellipse.

However for design work it is often unnecessary to be able to approximate an existing profile – more important is to have an analogy to a flexible curve which the designer can specify roughly and then modify interactively until he is happy with the result. Two main techniques are in widespread use in computer aided design: the first, due to P. Bézier of Renault, I shall describe and the second, called **B-splines**, I shall provide references for.

In many A-level mathematics syllabuses nowadays some vector geometry is included. One bit of theory frequently taught is the vector equation of a straight line. Suppose two points P_1 and P_2 have position vectors $\mathbf{p}_1$ and $\mathbf{p}_2$ relative to some origin 0. Then the position vector $\mathbf{r}$ of a point R on the line between P_1 and P_2 is given by

$$\mathbf{r} = (1 - t)\,\mathbf{p}_1 + t\mathbf{p}_2$$

where t is a parameter between 0 and 1. Here the vector $\mathbf{r}$ is a weighted average of the 2 vectors $\mathbf{p}_1$ and $\mathbf{p}_2$ where the 'weightlifting functions', $(1 - t)$ and t, are linear functions of the parameter t. It is a simple extension to think of generating a curve as the weighted average of the vectors of a set of n points $P_1, P_2, \ldots\ldots, P_n$ in which the weighting functions were $(n - 1)$th degree polynomials in the parameter t. This is exactly what Bézier does and he takes the terms of the branch of the binomial distribution function as his weighting functions. Thus for three points we have:

$$\mathbf{r} = (1 - t)^2\,\mathbf{p}_1 + 2(1 - t)t\,\mathbf{p}_2 + t^2\mathbf{p}_3$$

and for four points:

$$r = (1 - t)^3 p_1 + 3(1 - t)^2 t\, p_2 + 3(1 - t)t^2 p_3 + t^3 p_4$$

and in general, for n points:

$$r = \sum_{r=1}^{n-1} \binom{n-1}{r} (1 - t)^{n-1-r}\, t^r\, p_{r+1}$$

Thus in the following program we fit a curve to the N points whose screen coordinates are stored in the arrays X(I) and Y(I).

PROGRAM 4

```
100   N1 = N − 1
110   PLOT X(1), Y(1)
120   FOR T = 0.01 TO 0.99 STEP 0.01
130   T1 = T/(1 − T)
140   M = (1 − T)↑N1
150   SX = M * X(1)
160   SY = M * Y(1)
170   FOR I = 1 TO N1
180   M = M * (N − I) * T1/I
190   SX = SX + M * X(I + 1)
200   SY = SY + M * Y(I + 1)
210   NEXT I
220   LINE SX, SY
230   NEXT T
240   LINE X(N), Y(N)
```

It is quite possible to make this program more efficient but it does illustrate how the technique can be applied. The feature that is most apparent on displaying such a curve is that it only passes through the first and last points. In fact it starts tangential to the line $P_1 P_2$ and finishes tangential to the line $P_{n-1} P_n$. The points $P_2, P_3, \ldots, P_{n-1}$ are known as 'control points' and though the curve does not pass through them their positions serve to control the shape of the curve. With a little practice it becomes easy to guess where to place suitable control points to produce a desired effect. Then one or more control points can be moved so as to modify the resulting curve (see Fig. 10.4).

Whereas in the Bézier technique the whole curve is the weighted average of all the points in the B-spline technique the curve is composed of arcs each of which is, say, the weighted average of just 4 consecutive points where the weighting functions are carefully chosen so that the arcs join each other smoothly. For a reference to the technique see Newman and Sproull [1].

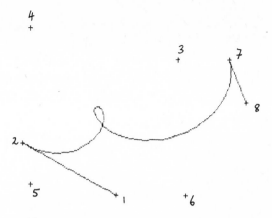

Fig. 10.4 – A Bézier curve generated by 8 points.

Solids

To represent solids the object space is, of course, three dimensional. Thus it is necessary (a) to maintain a description of the object − a 'data structure', (b) to be able to perform space transformations in 3D and (c) to project from the 3D object space to the 2D image space of the screen. The data structure needs to include (i) geometric information, for example, the space co-ordinates of the vertices (ii) topological information, for example, which vertices are joined by edges and, possibly, (iii) auxiliary display information such as which colour a particular edge is to be drawn in. At its simplest a solid object with plane faces can be described by 2 matrices: a $V \times 3$ matrix C giving the 3D coordinates of each of the body's V vertices and an $E \times 2$ matrix A giving for each of the E edges the numbers of the two vertices it joins.

A 3D transformation can be represented in a number of ways, but one common method is to use 4×4 matrices with homogeneous co-ordinates (see Oldknow [7]). Thus any combination of rotations, translations, stretches, shears and reflections can be applied to the matrix of co-ordinates C. In order to display the body it is necessary to choose a suitable form of projection. The simplest is orthographic projection in which one of the space-coordinates, for example, the Z co-ordinate, is ignored and the other two used to produce the screen coordinates directly. However it is quite easy to produce a perspective projection, which only requires the application of similar triangles. The derivation may be found in [7]. Suppose then that the matrix $C(I, J)$ holds the X, Y and Z co-ordinates of each of the V vertices and that the plane of the screen is taken as the XY-plane with the origin in the centre of the screen. Suppose, further, that the Z-axis comes out from the centre of the screen and that the eye is on the Z-axis at $(0,0,ZE)$ the following routine will draw a 'wire-frame' impression of the object described by the matrices C and A; the 'display-file' of screen coordinates is produced in matrix D.

PROGRAM 5

```
100  ZE = 1000: H = 160: K = 100
110  DIM D(100,2)
120  FOR I = 1 TO V
130  M = ZE/(ZE − C(I,3))
140  D(I,1) = M * C(I,1) + H
150  D(I,2) = M * C(I,2) + K
160  NEXT I
170  FOR I = 1 TO E
180  S = A(I,1): F = A(I,2)
190  PLOT D(S,1), D(S,2)
200  LINE D(F,1), D(F,2)
210  NEXT I
```

For a description of a technique for hidden-line removal (Fig. 10.5) see [7] and for details of a 3D manipulation package employing these techniques see Oldknow [8].

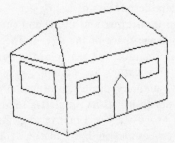

Fig. 10.5 − A perspective view of a house with hidden lines removed.

These, then, are a selection of the techniques useful for picture creation and manipulation in computer graphics. What follows is a description of some of their applications.

10.3 APPLICATIONS IN EDUCATION

Pupil programming

One of the most pleasurable features of writing programs for computer graphics is the immediate feedback − if you made a mistake in the program you can *see* straightaway that it failed to do what it was meant to. Another is its versatility − once you have a number of subroutines written to perform some of the basic drawing functions the ways these can be combined to create pleasing results are boundless and just depend upon the vision and creativity of the programmer. These attributes can be exploited in the classroom both to make programming appear as natural and important a mathematical skill as, say, the ability to use a calculator or a protractor, and also to generate an interest in geometry. Programming does not have to be an individual effort of one person sitting at one computer – graphics programming with one micro and a large screen is an ideal exercise. Of course the applicability of graphics programming goes far beyond the teaching of geometry – for example the ability to be able to display the graphs of functions has many uses within and outside mathematics teaching and histograms, pie charts and other visual presentations of statistics have many uses. However, for me, geometry is the most exciting area of application for it is often taught in a rather sterile, closed and abstract way and to have a dynamic medium for testing out ideas should be able to revitalise it.

Visualisation

Although there is a fair amount of attention given to solid geometry in most secondary school mathematics syllabuses there are considerable practical difficulties in organising practical classroom work to support it. For many children their ability to mentally manipulate space is determined by the time they leave primary school. Those children whose parents have showered them with constructional toys such as Lego, Meccano and Fischer Technik or who have been bitten by the construction kit bug have a head start in this respect. However, with a computer package that allows a pupil to manipulate a representation of a solid, such as a house, and to view it from many different viewpoints it is definitely possible to produce exercises that improve some children's spatial visualisation. One such package that I have produced with this application in mind has also been used for illustrating crystal structure in science teaching and with severely physically handicapped pupils to manipulate computer representations of objects that they are unable to physically manipulate.

Turtle

One very interesting aspect of using computers with children that is only just beginning to be exploited is that if the resulting output from an interactive program (usually a game) is stimulating and engrossing enough the child will easily come to grips with the operations he is required to perform to interact with the program. These operations (the 'moves' of the game) are dictated by the program designer and may be as mundane as just pressing one or two predefined buttons to make a spaceship zoom left or right but may equally be as sophisticated as requiring the player to specify the angle in degrees through which the ship is to turn. It is not necessary for the participant to be taught how angles are measured – he can pick this up from watching the behaviour of the graphics screen in response to his input – $10°$ may not be much of a turn but $100°$ is, what is more the ship always turns in the same sense (again predetermined by the designer) so there is a discovery to be made – how can we make the ship turn in the other direction? Some children will discover that $360°$ has something to do with it, others who might have come across negative numbers fiddling about with a calculator may come up with a different (but equivalent) solution. This is just a simple example of the potential of a totally new phenomenon in mathematical education — namely that children are now being brought up in the presence of 'maths-speaking' objects which (with subtle handling) they can learn to master in a similar way to learning to use a remote controller to work the TV set.

I have tried to exploit this idea in a package based upon ideas put forward by Seymour Papert [9] in which a child 'drives' a turtle around the screen by telling it how far to move and what angle to turn through. Although it is possible to 'program' the turtle by giving it a set of instructions that will not be obeyed until a particular key is pressed (much like the "Bigtrak" programmable toy) the package does not set out to teach as much about programming techniques as Papert's LOGO language. Its principal aim is to produce a satisfying drawing machine that can exercise children's abilities to estimate lengths and angles and encourage them to develop strategies for the production of complex patterns, see Fig. 10.6.

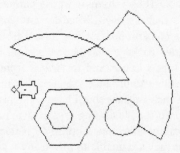

Fig. 10.6 — A pattern produced by a Turtle

At this point it is worthwhile interjecting a cautionary note: as previously mentioned some machines use pixels that are decidedly not square and unless the package designer tailors his mathematics to take account of this it is quite possible to display 'wrong' results. I have seen a CAL program, supposedly to help with giving a feel for angle, produce angles that were meant to be 90° which were clearly seen not to be right-angled. Similarly there is a program designed to help with transformation geometry, widely available for the teletext graphics of a particular machine, that shows a rotated square as a distinctly non-square rectangle. Such programs, however well designed in many respects, are worse than useless as they reinforce the opposite of the concepts that they are designed to teach. Usually such programs can be easily fixed by a little extra code but if they cannot be corrected they should be abandoned.

Computer Aided Design (CAD)
Computer systems have been developed that assist in many stages of the design and manufacture process. At Renault cars a body stylist can design body panels

for a new car in just the same way that I described for curve design. When he has a satisfactory design shown on the screen he can make the computer control a milling machine that will make a 3D model of his design. When a fully satisfactory design has been achieved the computer can produce all the engineering drawings needed on a plotter and can also produce the magnetic tapes to drive the numerically controlled machine tools that cut and shape the steel sheets. Computers can also carry out stress analyses and aerodynamic calculations and work is under way to link CAD techniques with the robotic production processes now in increasing use. With the dramatic reduction in costs of computing machinery computer aided design systems are being installed in relatively small industrial firms and there are strong signs that they will have much the same effect on traditional draughting skills as word processors are having on office skills.

In these circumstances it would seem reasonable that some taste of CAD techniques should find its way into craft, design and technology (CDT) teaching. No doubt it would be desirable in this work to have peripheral devices such as light pens and pen plotters but quite a lot can be achieved from keyboard and screen alone. One package I have produced simulates a commercial program produced by the Department of Industry's Computer Aided Design Centre in Cambridge for a company producing wine glasses. Here the user specifies the co-ordinates of a number of points on an imagined curve that represents the profile of the right hand side of the glass. The points are then joined by a smooth curve (a cubic spline) and the curve is then revolved about a vertical axis to give a three dimensional impression of the glass (Fig. 10.7). The initial points can then be changed by the user to adjust the design. Many of the current generations of relatively cheap dot-matrix printers are capable, albeit slowly, of producing a hard copy from the graphics screen memory, and so the design can be captured permanently. Although for industrial usage it is obviously preferable to specify the input points by pointing with a light pen at the screen I believe that the incidental reinforcement of other skills, such as the use of co-ordinates, is very valuable in an educational context.

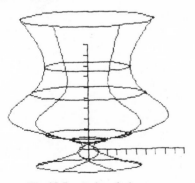

Fig. 10.7 – A glass design.

Art and design

The interactive use of computer graphics can have many applications in creative design work. For example it makes experimentation with perspective very easy and objects can be moved about the screen to explore composition. Some preliminary design work can be very tedious and time consuming — for example in 'pin-and-thread sculpture' (filography) thin coloured threads are woven between rows of nails. The spacing and position of the nails, the order in which they are threaded and the colours of the threads all effect the design. A package I have produced allows all these aspects to be experimented with until a pleasing design is reached from which it is then an easy matter to produce a physical model.

I have recently worked with a graphic artist, John Harries [10], who has adapted a notation, originally designed for whole-body choreography in ballet, for graphic art. In this a series of linkages each turn relative to one another — the whole resembling the movement of Durer's epicyclic compasses. This is an ideal representation of shape for computer application from which kinetic results can be achieved by filming or videotaping the shapes as they grow (see Fig. 10.8). Interest in this program has also been expressed by physical education teachers as it is easy to use this system to illustrate body movements such as swimming strokes or kicking actions.

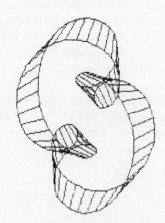

Fig. 10.8 – A design using the 'Shapes of Movement' notation.

Film production

The video output from a microcomputer can just as easily be fed into a video recorder as to a TV. Thus computer generated images can be recorded and subsequently edited. A soundtrack can be dubbed over and the computer graphics interspersed with filmed images to make educational film materials. Direct photography from the monitor screen can also be used to produce complex overhead projector transparencies which would be too difficult to produce by conventional means.

10.4 POSTSCRIPT

I have given examples of just a few of the techniques and applications of computer graphics but its potential for education is vast. However one should not lose sight of the changes that microelectronic technology is bringing about in the world outside education, particularly in the field of employment. As traditional 'middle man' skills such as printing, film processing, typing and draughting are undermined, it is the creative skills of the journalist, producer, author and designer that become of ever increasing importance and to this end it is obvious that the educational system needs to adapt to the changes. It is undoubtedly capable of providing non-vocational skills, but what is essential is a change in attitude to teaching and learning where such skills are not seen as just a preparation for the higher education of an academic minority but an important aspect of the preparation of an adaptable new generation of adults.

REFERENCES

[1] Newman, W. M. and Sproull, R. F., (1979), *Principles of Interactive Computer Graphics*, (2nd ed.), Mc Graw-Hill, New York.

[2] Bresenham, J. E., (1965), 'Algorithm for Computer Control of a Digital Plotter', *IBM Syst. J.*, 4(1), 25-30.

[3] Pitteway, M. L. V., (1979), 'Algorithm for Drawing Ellipses or Hyperbolae with a Digital Plotter', *Comput. J.*, 10(3), 282-289, November.

[4] Gossling, T. H., (1981), 'Bulge, shear and squash: a representation for the general conic arc', *Computer-aided design*, 13(2), 81-84, March.

[5] Lockwood, E. H., (1970), *A Book of Curves*, Cambridge.

[6] Greville, T. N. E., (1968), *Theory and applications of spline functions*, Academic Press, London.

[7] Oldknow, A. J., (1974), 'Motion Geometry in Action', *Mathematics Teaching*, 67, 48-51, June.

[8] Oldknow, A. J., (1980), '3D graphics for 380Z, PET and Apple', *Computers in School*, 3(2)., 6-9, December.

[9] Papert, S., (1980), *Mindstorms: Children, Computers and Powerful Ideas*, Harvester Press, 1980.

[10] Harries, J. G., (1969), *Shapes of Movement*, Movement Notation Society, Tel Aviv.

Appendix 1 — Versions of programs 1-5 to run on a Research Machines 380Z with high resolution graphics.

```
50 REM PROGRAM 1 OF PET-IN-ED
55 REM A 'CIRCLE' WITH SNAGS
60 REM A.J.OLDKNOW,  9.9.81
90 CALL "RESOLUTION",0,2
100 R=75:R2=R*R
110 FOR X=-R TO R
120 Y=SQR(R2-X*X)
130 CALL "PLOT",X+160,100+Y,3
140 CALL "PLOT",X+160,100-Y
150 NEXT X
```

```
50 REM PROGRAM 2 OF PET-IN-ED
55 REM A PARAMETRIC 'CIRCLE'
60 REM A.J.OLDKNOW,  9.9.81
90 CALL "RESOLUTION",0,2
100 R=75:N=40:DA=8*ATN(1)/N
120 CALL "PLOT",R+160,100
130 FOR A=DA TO 6.3 STEP DA
140 X=R*COS(A)
150 Y=R*SIN(A)
160 CALL "LINE",X+160,Y+100
170 NEXT A
```

```
50 REM PROGRAM 3 OF PET-IN-ED
55 REM A CIRCLE GENERATED BY ROTATIONS
60 REM A.J.OLDKNOW,  9.9.81
90 CALL "RESOLUTION",0,2
100 H=160:K=100:R=75:N=40
110 A=8*ATN(1)/N:XS=1.1
120 X=R:Y=0:S=SIN(A):C=COS(A)
130 CALL "PLOT",X*XS+H,K
140 FOR I=1 TO N
150 XT=X*C-Y*S
160 Y=X*S+Y*C
170 X=XT
180 CALL "LINE",X*XS+H,Y+K
190 NEXT I
```

```
50 REM PROGRAM 4 OF PET-IN-ED
60 REM A.J.OLDKNOW,  9.9.81
65 REM SET UP ARRAYS OF CONTROL POINTS
70 N=10:DIM X(10),Y(10):FOR I=1 TO N
80 X(I)=30*I:READ Y(I):NEXT I
85 DATA 50,100,30,90,160,120,180,70,10,40
90 CALL "RESOLUTION",0,2
92 REM DISPLAY THE CONTROL POINTS
95 FOR I=1 TO N:CALL"PLOT",X(I)-2,Y(I),2:CALL"LINE",X(I)+2,Y(I)
96 CALL "PLOT",X(I),Y(I)-2:CALL"LINE",X(I),Y(I)+2:NEXT I
100 N1=N-1
110 CALL "PLOT",X(1),Y(1),3
120 FOR T=0.01 TO 0.99 STEP 0.01
130 T1=T/(1-T)
140 M=(1-T)↑N1
150 SX=M*X(1)
160 SY=M*Y(1)
170 FOR I=1 TO N1
180 M=M*(N-I)*T1/I
190 SX=SX+M*X(I+1)
200 SY=SY+M*Y(I+1)
210 NEXT I
220 CALL "LINE",SX,SY
230 NEXT T
240 CALL "LINE",X(N),Y(N)
```

```
50 REM PROGRAM 5 OF PET-IN-ED
55 REM A 3D PROJECTION
60 REM A.J.OLDKNOW,  9.9.81
65 REM SET UP DATA FOR A TRIANGULAR PRISM
70 V=6:E=9:DIM C(6,3),A(9,2)
72 REM FIRST READ IN THE VERTEX CO-ORDINATES
75 FOR I=1 TO V:FOR J=1 TO 3:READ C(I,J):NEXT J:NEXT I
76 DATA 100,-40,70,100,80,0,100,-40,-70,-100,-40,70,-100,80,0,-100,-40,-70
78 REM NOW READ IN THE INCIDENCE MATRIX OF VERTICES ON EDGES
80 FOR I=1 TO E:FOR J=1 TO 2:READ A(I,J):NEXT J:NEXT I
85 DATA 1,2,2,3,3,1,1,4,4,5,5,6,6,4,5,2,6,3
90 CALL "RESOLUTION",0,2
100 ZE=1000:H=160:K=100
110 DIM D(V,2)
120 FOR I=1 TO V
130 M=ZE/(ZE-C(I,3))
140 D(I,1)=M*C(I,1)+H
150 D(I,2)=M*C(I,2)+K
160 NEXT I
170 FOR I=1 TO E
180 S=A(I,1):F=A(I,2)
190 CALL "PLOT",D(S,1),D(S,2),3
200 CALL "LINE",D(F,1),D(F,2)
210 NEXT I
```

CHAPTER 11

A versatile double-density plotting and screen to hardcopy package for CAL

David Williams, Brunel University, Uxbridge, Middlesex

11.1 THE NEED FOR MACHINE-CODE PLOT AND PRINT ROUTINES

For the past couple of years I have been modifying the Biology programs of the Chelsea Science Simulation Project and the Schools Council Computers in the Curriculum Project to run on the various versions of the PET. The original programs were designed to produce output on a teletype, but in a number of cases advantage has been taken of the PET display to show proper graphs by POKEing the screen memory. Such displays cannot easily be generated directly on to a lineprinter, especially if double-density plotting using the quarter-square graphics characters is employed. From my own experience of using CAL programs and from the comments of colleagues I felt that the facility of hard copy production was highly desirable. Therefore a simple screen-to-printer routine was added to early versions. Written in BASIC, it took about five seconds per line to perform the screen-PEEK to CBM-'ASCII' code conversion, and it soon became tedious to use. The alternative was a machine-coded routine, much quicker and also more compact especially if it could make use of BASIC interpreter ROM routines. A number of the Chelsea programs had already been squeezed from more than 13k bytes to run on a PET with 7k of user RAM, so space was at a premium. For similar reasons of speed and efficient use of memory, a machine-coded double density plotting routine, adapted from A. Clark (*Practical Computing* July 1979), was used where required. It was also decided that the code should be attached directly to the program since using a BASIC loader to assemble the routines from DATA statements would also make heavy demands on memory space.

Where, then, should the routines go? They might go into the second cassette buffer and be saved as a contiguous unit with BASIC using the machine language monitor to start at $033A instead of $0400. But the programs were intended for wide distribution and it was envisaged that computer non-specialists making copies for their class use by simple SAVEing would lose the machine code and gain a lot of frustration. Since some users would need to load programs from tape, the first cassette buffer was not available for those using both routines.

What about leaving them at the top end of the BASIC program? With twenty or more programs each using the routines, and each periodically being updated, keeping track of the addresses for SYS (or USR) links might be a problem. The routines would still take up valuable memory on a small machine.

The solution was to attach them to the BASIC programs in user RAM, but *after* loading to move them into the cassette buffers, freeing working space for variables and arrays. This approach took on greater significance when versions of BASIC began to multiply.

As Commodore continue to change their range of computers, the writer of programs which access the Read-Only-Memory routines of the BASIC interpreter finds it necessary to produce a number of versions of his software. So far we have BASIC 1.0 (old-ROM), BASIC 2.0 (new-ROM), and BASIC 4.0 with its variants for 40 column 9 inch and 12 inch screens and the 8032. There are 8k, 16k and 32k machines. Since the routines here developed were to be relocated to a fixed position in RAM regardless of the size of the BASIC program or total user memory, it was possible to change references to ROM easily if necessary after relocation. However because of the added complication of a different operating system scratch-pad in page zero of RAM it was finally decided that BASIC 1.0 would not be supported.

11.2 LOADING THE PACKAGE

Attaching the routines to a BASIC program is achieved by an extra relocation routine. PACK32N.S is the source file for a package of subroutines loaded into high memory. Once loaded and protected by moving the top of memory down, the BASIC program is loaded in the usual way. The command SYS32000 moves everything from $7A8F to $7CFF to the end of the BASIC and moves pointers in the operating system so that the whole may be SAVEd and reloaded in the normal way. SYS32015 moves all except the double-density plotter.

If required, versions based at 16000 or 8000 could be assembled for preparing programs on machines with less memory.

To use the routines, the BASIC program must begin with lines 2 and 4 of SCR-PR-BASIC (Fig. 11.1), which work as follows: the first SYS call is to the PET identification routine. This halts with an error message if BASIC 1.0 is found. On an 80 column PET it sets the left margin to give a centralised 40 column display. The screen width is stored in a spare page zero location 162. The keyboard buffer is primed with 'home-cursor' and 'carriage return's'. The next SYS call relocated the screen-to-printer routine to cassette buffer 2 starting at location 826. If called on a BASIC 2.0 machine the BASIC 4.0 ROM entry addresses are amended. The SYS call in line 4 does likewise for the double-density plotter, moved to cassette buffer 1. This call should be deleted if the plotter is not included.

The second half of line 4 clears the screen and prints line numbers and RUN on successive lines. At END the PET takes characters from the keyboard buffer put there by the identification routine, thus deleting lines 2 and 4 and starting the main program. Had those lines remained, a subsequent RUN would crash the PET attempting to access non-existent relocation routines.

```
SCR-PR-BASIC

TOTAL PROGRAM MEMORY USED = 283 BYTES


2 print"[clr]" sys(peek(42)+256*peek(43)-145):sys(peek(42)+
  256*peek(43))826
4 sys(peek(42)+256*peek(43)+170)634:print"[u/c][clr]2[crd]4
  [crd]run":end
100 :
150 :
178 sys(634)int((yo+y)*256)+xo+x-40*(peek(162)=80)
200 :
250 :
284 cc=18:open4,4:print#4:gosub292
286 forj=2to25:ifj=23thencc=30:gosub292
288 sys(826)j
290 next:close4:cc=24
292 open6,4,6:print#6,chr$(cc+pr):close6:return
300 end


Control codes:  listed in square brackets

clr = clear screen;  equivalent to CHR$(147)

u/c = close up display on 12" screens;  equivalent to CHR$(142)
           (ignored by PETs with 9" screens)

crd = cursor down· equivalent to CHR$(17)
```

Fig. 11. 1 – BASIC program, SCR-PR-BASIC, for using the package.

11.3 USING THE PLOT AND PRINT ROUTINES

The other representative lines of BASIC in Fig. 11.1 show the communication with the plotter and screen-transfer routines.

Line 178 requires the origin coordinates XO and YO on the 80 × 50 plotting grid with reference to the bottom left corner of the display (n.b. not the same as the screen on 80 column PETs). X and Y are the coordinates of the point to be plotted. Subtracting 128 from the expression ($YO + Y$) causes the point to be plotted black (erased). The latter negative part of the expression ensures a central plot on an 80 column screen.

Subroutines starting at line 284 show an advantage of the screen being transferred line by line. In this example screen line 1, the top line, is not transferred. A block of lines from any part of the display could easily be selected. It is

A block of lines from any part of the display could easily be selected. It is possible, by POKEs to locations 879, 979 and 980 after relocation, to alter the left and right screen limits of the block. Line spacing on a CBM printer may be altered in the middle of a block to give, for example, continuous graphs with well separated legends on the bottom lines (see Fig. 11.2).

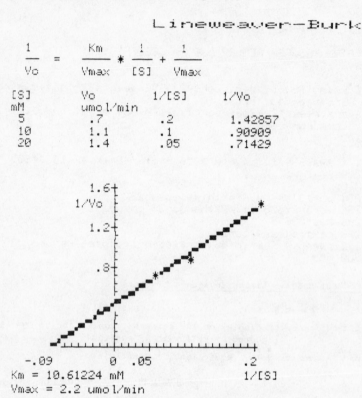

Fig. 11.2 – Example of use of package with a program showing solutions to the Michaelis-Menton equation.

I believe that the use of lowercase printing where possible greatly improves the legibility of a crowded display. The code conversion in the screen-to-printer routine assume such a display. The default condition converts screen PEEK code to CBM-'ASCII' and allows for some oddities in the CBM printer when required to print CHR$(91) to CHR$(95) while in lowercase mode. An alternative is available to provide true ASCII to a non-Commodore printer via an IEEE-RS232C interface. Location 879 should be POKEd with 53 before printing to obtain this type of output. My elderly IEEE-RS232C interface was designed for use with an old-ROM PET 2001 so a small amendment is needed to handle its different upper/lowercase convention.

In summary, a package is presented containing a pair of useful and versatile routines which combine the speed, efficiency and compact size of machine code using ROM routines, ease of attachment to BASIC and the portability of machine-independent BASIC programs. Copies of the machine code programs are available on request to the author.

CHAPTER 12

PETNET – data transmission system

Nick Green, Commodore Business Machines (UK), Slough, Berkshire

---

PETNET is a data transmission system currently running at 300 baud for PET-to-PET and PET-to-mainframe communication.

The PETNET mainframe host is configured as a richly fed back, hierarchically tree-structured database for the storage and retrieval of user-originated information. The system has been designed by the Special Projects Department of CBM (UK) Limited and implemented by Ariadne Software Limited with ADP Limited providing host facilities.

At the time of writing, the system is in the preliminary testing phase.

12.1 THE CONCEPT OF PETNET

Information on PETNET can be thought of as a hierarchy of nodes which may be program or data. The term 'description' may usefully be used.

This hierarchy of descriptions may be used to represent a piece of knowledge about the real world and as such may find applications for both teaching and information retrieval. The limitations of trees of data of this kind are not fully understood yet but it is felt that a wide range of applications exist and the potential for simplifying management and presentation of real world information seems very large. The system is like Prestel in the structure of its data base but quite different in the way in which nodes or pages of information are manipulated.

Firstly, users are able to input information as easily as they can retrieve it. Secondly, users can send comments to existing entries with a view to rendering applications self-organising. The continuing growth of the system is ensured by a death date associated with each item. It is hoped that this will give an environment which will aid the development of each item and which could be compared with a medieval market place or an electronic exchange and mart.

Each item on the system has a death data associated with it at which time the item will be deleted unless the author chooses one of the following options:

(1) To extend the lifetime for an additional period.
(2) To replace the item by a new version, revised and up-dated in the light of user reaction.

It is to be hoped that most authors will choose the second of these options, giving a dynamic and steadily improving system.

What most distinguishes PETNET from all other such systems is the amount of feedback and user interaction anticipated. This falls into three main divisions:

(1) The directory structure is under user control in that uploading can be to any free node in the overall tree. Those areas of wide interest in the system can be expected to grow, whilst areas of little interest may die off the system completely.
(2) A particular form of uploading is the appending of comments to items placed on the system by other authors. These would generally take the form of suggestions for improvements or developments. Comments reside on the system until the death date of the item to which they are attached, at which time it is to be hoped that the authors will extend or update his entry in response to this user feedback.
(3) As an aid to selection of items, a user can examine associated comment files. A simple indication of status is provided in the directory in the form of a satisfaction index (USI) which is a digit from 1–9 representing an average user vote on the item in question. Users other than the author may exercise a right to vote at any time.

It is hoped at some further stage to go into the cybernetics of this design. The work of Beer and Pask has been used most in the creation of this design.

In the following sections, we discuss briefly the data transmission protocol used, the features of the user terminal, host software organisation and the likely availability of the PETNET service.

12.2 DATA TRANSMISSION PROTOCOL

A packeted data transmission protocol has been adopted. This will fit into other authorities data transmission schemes but, at the moment, this packet link operates only at 300 baud asynchronously and over Public Switch Telephone Network subscriber lines.

The need was to propose a protocol that would give a very high measure of error-free data transmission, without reducing the speed received by the user much below the rather slow 300 baud.

A polynomial error check technique was used and the packet structure is outlined below.

sop   char count   type   seq no   .... data ....   crc1   crc2   eop

sop	Start of packet character $01 — occurs nowhere else in packet.
char count	Total number of characters in packet, consisting of single bytes, or the control character CVB (change value byte) + byte pairs.
type	Single character packet type, as detailed below.
seq no	Sequence number from $20 to $50, used to identify packet for acknowledgement purposes, and to allow files to be assembled in correct sequence. Two sets of packet sequence numbers will be maintained, for transmission and for reception.
data	1 to 57 characters of binary data.
crc1 crc2	2 character cyclic redundancy check word over packet from character count up to end of data.
eop	End of packet — special interrupt character $02, used to tell multiplexer to pass packet to mainframe. Occurs nowhere else in packet.

At any one time several packets may be in flight to the user unacknowledged. This is because at present PETNET host software is regarded by its mainframe as a job to be swopped in and swopped out. This could imply an up to two second delay before a handshake for a correctly received packet would be processed by the host. Thus, to reduce apparent delays to the user, up to four packets are sent at any one time without handshake. A numbered ACK packet is sent to indicate error free representation of each one of the currently active quartet of packets.

It is to be hoped that standards in this area will make progress and we look forward to appropriate international recommendations to be made soon. There are a number of bodies who have currently made recommendations, for example File Transfer Protocol Implementors Group, Data Communications Protocol Unit, National Physical Laboratory (1981) but these recommendations seldom go to the detail required for applications such as this. The resulting packet has a very high noise immunity and up to now this author can state that throughout testing on the system no undetected errors have been observed.

Users can therefore reasonably expect that any file being transferred using the system may at times be transmitted somewhat slowly but will be transmitted without error.

12.3 TERMINAL FEATURES

Entering the environment

The PETNET software must be loaded off disk or tape and run. When this is done, the following happens:

(1) The screen clears and displays PETNET in a large character display. Underneath is:

PETNET loaded.
You have the following new direct mode commands:
EDITOR – enters the PETNET frame editor.
LOGON – initiates communication with PETNET host.
COMMENT – alters function of stop key to allow a comment frame on a downloaded program to be built up.
NOCOMMENT – kills the COMMENT facility.
RESET – resets the PET.

(2) The rest of the PETNET code relocates to the top of memory, and page 0 pointers are altered to protect it.

(3) The CHRGET routine on page 0 is altered to scan for the new commands listed above.

At this stage, if the user does not use any of the extra commands, the PET can be used to enter, edit and run programs as usual, but with a few K less memory space available. Alternatively, he has two main options:

(1) Issuing the EDITOR command, which transfers to the frame editing environment, allowing him to prepare material for later uploading to the PETNET host.

(2) Issuing the LOGON command, which initiates the log on procedure to the PETNET host.

The COMMENT and NOCOMMENT commands would not normally be used unless a program had already been downloaded from the PETNET host.

Editing environment

As part of the relocation procedure, the PETNET software will reserve 1k of memory at the top of RAM to act as a storage area for PETNET frames, while not actually displayed on the screen. This allows rapid transfer between the frame being worked on, and a 'command screen' giving a menu of choices for editing, etc. This 1k reserved area will be referred to as 'frame space'.

The direct-mode command EDITOR causes an immediate display of the editor command screen, which is as follows:

f　display current frame
s　save current frame to disk
g　get frame from disk
p　dump frame to printer
c　clear current frame
l　log on to host
x　exit to basic

If the user presses one of these keys, the system responds as follows:

f　the current contents of frame space are transferred to screen RAM, and a flashing cursor is displayed at the top left. The user can now employ the PETNET screen editor as explained below.

s　the screen is cleared, and the user asked to supply a drive number and a file name (the system will not respond to invalid drive numbers or to efforts to enter more than 16 character file names). The current frame is saved to disk in compacted (space-crunched) form, followed by a transfer back to the command screen. In the event of a disk error, an error message is displayed, and the user given the option to abort, or to initialise the drive and try again.

g　the screen is cleared, and the user asked to supply a drive number and file name as above. The frame specified is then loaded into frame space followed by a return to the command screen, or else an error message is displayed as above.

p　the current contents of frame space are dumped on a Commodore printer.

c　the screen is cleared, and the message displayed 'clear frame from memory — are you sure?'. If the user presses the 'y' key, frame space is cleared, followed by a transfer back to the command screen. Any other key causes a transfer back to the command screen, with no other action taking place.

l　a transfer is made to the PETNET log on procedure.

x　a transfer is made back to BASIC. The current contents of frame space are retained, unless the user enters COMMENT mode.

The PETNET screen editor
The following will be available for screen editing. All keys, including cursor control keys, function exactly as in the normal PET BASIC editor, with the following exceptions.

(1) The RUN/STOP key causes the current screen contents to be saved in frame space, followed by a transfer to the editor command screen.

(2) The CLR key will not function to clear the screen. (To do this, the user must use RUN/STOP to transfer to the command screen, then use the clear frame option).

(3) The bottom line is reserved for the current file name, if appropriate. It is not possible to cursor down into this line and screen scroll is disabled.

(4) The @ key has a control function:

> @ followed by @ prints an @ sign
> @ followed by DEL performs line delete with scroll-up
> @ followed by INST performs line insert with scroll-down
> @ followed by 'r' enables automatic repeat on all keys
> @ followed by 'o' switches of repeat on all keys
> @ followed by 'h' displays help screen, explaining screen editor commands.

Log on procedure

The log on procedure can be initiated from BASIC by the LOGON command, or from the editor command screen by the 'l' option.

(1) Dial-up instructions appear on the screen as follows:

> PETNET log on
>
> Switch modem to originate (or) and full duplex (fd).
> Dial into the host system.
> Wait for a continuous high tone.
> Press receiver into modem with cord at end indicated.
> Check that the CRX light comes on.
>
> If successful, press l to continue with log on.
> Otherwise, press b to return to BASIC,
> or press e to return to editor.

If 'b' or 'e' is pressed, the corresponding jump is made.
If 'l' is pressed, log on continues as follows.

(2) The screen is cleared and the user is asked to input his ID, followed by his password. The host sends back a command block accepting or rejecting the log on.

    If the log on is rejected, the screen clears and the message is displayed 'log on rejected – incorrect password'. The user is then given the options to try again, or to exit to BASIC or to the editor. In the latter cases, a 'transaction complete' command block is sent to the host, followed by the appropriate jump in the PET software.

    After three unsuccessful trials, transaction complete is sent, a 'line disconnected' message is displayed and the user is returned to (1) either to re-dial or to exit to BASIC or to the editor.

If the log on is accepted dialog continues as in (3) below.

(3) The host sends one or more command blocks containing the following information:

    (a) The user's name.

    (b) The date of last access.

    (c) The pages the user has on the system.

    (d) The pages within one week of death.

(4) When the user presses space, the PETNET command screen is immediately displayed, and the system proceeds as detailed below.

PETNET command screen

The PETNET command screen is displayed immediately following log on, and can be returned to at a later stage by pressing RUN/STOP as detailed below. The command screen is as follows:

    d   examine directory

    g   go to specified page number

    a   examine state of user account

    c   catalogue user pages on system

    n   catalogue user pages near death

    e   exit to editor

    b   exit to BASIC

The current page directory entry is displayed in reverse field on the bottom line if appropriate.

If the user presses one of these keys, the system responds as follows:

    d   the PET sends a command block requesting directory information for the current page number (000000 if the user has just logged on). The host sends back one or more command blocks containing this information, which is then displayed on the screen, etc, as described below.

    g   the screen clears and the user is asked to input a system page number which must be six characters in length. The PET then sends a command block requesting directory information for the specified page number. The host sends the specified directory information, or else sends a command block indicating that no such page exists. The PET displays the directory, etc, as described below, or else gives a 'no such page' error message, followed by a return to the command screen.

    a   the PET sends a command block requesting account information. The host sends back a command block containing this information, which is displayed on a clear screen, followed by a return to the command screen.

c   the screen clears, and the user is asked to specify screen or printer. The PET sends the host a command block requesting all directory entries associated with the user. The host sends back command blocks containing this information, which the PET directs to screen or printer as required. The system then returns to the command screen.

n   the PET requests and the host sends directory entries for pages within a week of death, with a screen/printer option as above.

e   the PET sends a transaction complete command block to the host, then exits to the editor command screen.

b   the PET sends transaction complete, then exits to BASIC.

12.4 MAINFRAME FUNCTIONS

Directory environment

Following a request for directory information the screen clears, and the information received from the host is displayed as a sequence of entries of the following format:

nnnnnn   tttttttttttttttt x ppp.pp i ddmmyy

where

nnnnnn is the system page ID
tttttttttttttttt is the page title
x is the page type (d=directory, m=mail, p=program, c=comment)
ppp.pp is the price
i is the user satisfaction index
ddmmyy is the expiry date of the page

At the bottom of the screen, the directory information for the current page is displayed in the same format, in reverse field.
The user has the following options:

(1) The cursor up (and down) keys can be used to move the band of reverse field off the bottom line, and onto another directory entry.
(2) Pressing carriage return causes the PET to send a directory request command block for the page indicated by the reverse field line. The host then sends the specified directory information, which is displayed as above.
(3) Pressing d causes the PET to send a download request command block for the page indicated by the reverse-field line (unless the page is of directory type). The downloading process then takes place as described below.
(4) Pressing u causes the reverse field line to move to a blank line and a cursor to appear at the start of the page title field. The user is allowed to enter a title of up to 12 characters followed by the return key. The cursor then moves to allow the user to input page type, price and expiry date in the same way.

(5) Pressing v allows the user to vote on the page indicated by the reverse field line. The screen clears, and the message 'voting on' followed by the relevant page directory entry is displayed. The user is then asked to input a number from 1 to 9. The PET sends the host a 'vote' command block, containing the frame ID and the vote. The system then returns either to the command screen or to the last directory display.

(6) Pressing RUN/STOP causes the command screen to be displayed.

It might be desirable to list these options at the top of the screen.

Downloading procedure
After the PET has sent a download request command, the procedure followed depends on the page type, as detailed below:

Mail and comment downloading procedure

(1) The PET checks for the presence of a disk drive. If there is one, the user is given the options of downloading to screen only, or to screen and disk drive.

(2) The host sends block of 8-bit screen code containing the (compacted) screen information. This is displayed on the screen and stored in frame space, and simultaneously output to disk if this option has been chosen. The corresponding directory entry is displayed at the bottom of the screen.

(3) Following the downloading, pressing RUN/STOP causes a transfer to the command screen.

Program downloading procedure

(1) The host sends a block containing the program start and end addresses.

(2) The PET check if these addresses are available, and whether or not there is a disk drive present. The software then chooses one of the following possibilities:

   (a) If neither RAM nor disk is available, the system prints 'No room in RAM — disk drive needed' and sends an 'abort' command block to the host. It then exits to the command screen.

   (b) If there is RAM available but no disk drive, an 'okay' command block is sent to the host. The host then sends blocks of 8-bit program code, which are stored in RAM, starting at the address specified. The system then exists to the command screen.

   (c) If RAM is not available, but disks are present, the user is told 'No room in RAM — download to disk'. Depending on a 'y' or 'n' response an abort or an okay command block is sent to the host. If abort is sent the PET exits to the command screen immediately, otherwise the host sends blocks of 8-bit program code, which are output to the disk drive, followed by an exit to the command screen.

(d) If RAM and disk are available, the user is given the choice of down-loading to either, or to both. Downloading then proceeds as appropriate.

Uploading procedure
Following the input of new directory information, the screen clears and the screen displays 'Uploading' followed by the new directory entry. The system then checks for a disk drive; if present the user is given the option of uploading from RAM or from disk. A check is then made to see if the relevant information is actually present in RAM or on disk. If not, the system exits to the command frame; otherwise uploading proceeds as follows:

(1) The PET sends a 'page create' command block, containing current page ID followed by the new directory information.

(2) The PET then sends 8-bit program or mail blocks. Programs are preceded by their start and end addresses.

(3) The system then returns to the command frame.

The COMMENT and NOCOMMENT options
The COMMENT direct mode command alters the function of the STOP key as follows:

If stop is pressed while a BASIC program is running, a two line window opens at the top of the screen, and a flashing cursor is displayed. The user can enter up to a total of 24 lines, which are stored in frame space for later editing/sending to PETNET as a comment page.

If stop is pressed again while the window is open, it functions as a normal BASIC stop.

If return is pressed twice in succession, the window is closed, and program execution continues.

The NOCOMMENT command disables this facility.

12.5 OPERATION OF THE SYSTEM AND APPLICATIONS
Host features
At the time of writing, the host software is currently being implemented in a not particularly portable FORTRAN. The host software will manage directory, informing particular users of the pages they have created and any pages they have that may be 'near to death'.

Housekeeping software, deleting unpaid for files and preparing the near to death report, will be run at night.

Billing records are also kept.

Tariff philosophy

Users entering information will be charged at minimum on a kilobyte per day basis. We hope always to keep these costs extremely low and this money will be directly payable to Commodore, who will in turn make payments to the host supplier.

Users wishing to retrieve this information will be charged at a rate determined by the the originating user, up to £999.99. Expensive software could not be downloaded unless dongal style or equivalent hardware protection is available.

Users opening accounts will require a credit card number and billing will be monthly or quarterly depending on the amount of transactions involved. Commodore will take a commission from originators selling information over the system.

International availability

Comunication links exist with most countries and it is likely that an international service will be offered before too long.

PTT regulations vary from country to country and we are seeking clarification on the kind of international service that PETNET users can expect.

Applications

It is difficult to foresee all the applications a system of this kind can support but some include dealer and user software and hardware support, user-to-user communications, dealer-to-user and user-to-dealer transactions. We hope many people will offer software information services on this system and with the storage costs at a minimum, we expect such a service to be offered to end users at low cost. We anticipate that the system will be extended to VIC users as soon as feasible. With the coming of the VIC, one sees a very large number of naive or first time users who will require a non-fuss and no-frills support that only PETNET can instantaneously offer.

We look forward to supporting VIC users in this way.

Education

It is hoped that educational users will play a major part in the development of the PETNET database. We hope that the availability of the system will be of use to teachers requiring public domain or local software for use in the class. The tree structure of the directory will make it easy to identify quickly areas of interest on the system, with an option for immediate downloading of useful items. It is also hoped that the use of USI's and comment facilities will aid the continuing development of educational software and help get away from a tendency for teacher/authors to expound considerable energy 're-inventing the wheel'. Additionally, the system can be used as an educational bulletin board for requests for information, notification of meetings, useful discoveries, etc. It could be the vehicle for massive curriculum software development starting off by collecting topic lists for particular subject matters and when these lists are agreed, proceeding to a program writing phase.

ACKNOWLEDGEMENT

Most of the details in this article have been taken from material prepared by Ariadne Software.

My thanks to Dave Parkinson and Mike Bolley of that company for their support and help and my thanks to Commodore Business Machines for permission to publish details of the system.

Any enquiries about PETNET should be addressed to Commodore Business Machines, 675 Ajax Avenue, Slough.

CHAPTER 13

The use of microcomputers to control equipment

Peter Avis, The Anthony Gell School, Wirksworth, Derbyshire

Fig. 13.1 – Ian Minion (3rd year) with his computer controlled crane.

13.1 WHAT IS COMPUTER CONTROL?

The popularity of computers at the present time comes from both pupils' and teachers' awareness of the change microelectronic technology will make on our society. This is linked with pupils finding computers both exciting and enjoyable.

Most computer studies courses cover programming, data processing, the structure of computers etc. Very few schools at the moment look at how computers can be used to control equipment such as motors, lights etc. in a practical way.

This is a pity since there are good educational reasons for exploring this field. Firstly I want to explain precisely what I mean by computer control.

The computer, however it is used, is primarily a device for controlling electrical signals. Whether it is sending electrical signals to operate a printer or a tape drive it is acting as a controller. There are numerous applications in industry where the computer is used to control other external devices. Computers control assembly lines, welding robots, cutting devices as well as monitoring signals from experimental rigs, electronic systems in cars etc. This is besides the use of dedicated microprocessors and other microelectronics to perform all sorts of control applications in various devices. In this article I will use the term 'Computer' to mean anything that can be programmed to process data. Various schools have different types of computer to explore 'Computer Control'. In principle it matters very little whether this is done on a minicomputer, a microcomputer a single board microprocessor system or a three chip controller. There has been some notable pioneering work in this field by teachers like Peter Nicholls at Belper School and Graham Thorpe at Rowlinson School. These and several others have demonstrated the educational value of control applications in school for all ages and abilities.

13.2 WHY INTRODUCE CONTROL BY COMPUTER?

I would urge teachers to explore the ways they can introduce this aspect into their teaching for the following reasons:

(1) It explains about the real world

Schools have a duty to explain about the real world. The scientist and the mathematician should relate their subjects to what is happening outside the classroom. In the same way the teacher talking about computers and micro-electronics cannot ignore the likelihood that computers and microprocessors will be heavily used in the future for controlling machinery. This is recognised by the British Computer Society who place the automatic control of processes as the first of their list of what schools should be teaching in the future [1]. This argument that we should teach it just because it is there will not be so easily accepted. After all we do not teach about cars, television, etc in schools to any great extent and it is a sensible question to ask whether these are less important than microprocessors. The possible answer to this question is to ask another question — are we satisfied with the way people use cars, television etc given the *ad hoc* way they have been educated in their use? I would argue that schools have a duty to prepare pupils for a life which will be greatly affected by microelectronic control, essentially because it will be a vastly different future to the present day situation. Could even the most cynical of people in the early fifties have predicted the average night of television viewing thirty years later? Does the example of television predict that the microelectronic revolution will produce a vast entertainment industry tied together with a whole commercial empire for selling trivia. What will be the *Blankety Blank* and TV commercials of the microelectronics industry?

It is possible to argue that television programmes are so poor because the average viewer expects and wants no better, but this surely must be where education has so much to offer. Education must widen people's horizons so that they experience using microelectronics for their own advantage rather than act purely as passive receivers. Schools can do this by encouraging pupils to write their own programs to control their own machines as well as talking about prepackaged microelectronic gadgets.

(2) It is true problem solving

Perhaps another strong reason for involving computer control in the school curriculum is to look at computers from a purely educational point of view. Asking pupils to program computers is one of the very few problem solving tasks which can be succesfully tackled in schools. Much of what we teach obscures the need to solve a realistic problem from scratch. As a mathematics teacher I know that much of what I teach will not be of use to pupils and yet mathematics is directly related to solving problems. In the many years that mathematics has been on the school syllabus it has not been able to free itself from the image of meaningless rules, formulae to learn, and boring repetitive manipulation. If computer studies is not to go down the same road, then we must ensure that it concentrates on using the computer to solve relevant problems – and the problems should be relevant to the pupil, not necessarily to the teacher, examination board or to local industry. Having programmed the computer to produce one million cube roots, a thousand "I HATE NOTTINGHAM FOREST", a hundred addresses, and ten failed space invader games, the pupil will begin to ask – Where next? The obvious answer which demonstrates the use of the computer and highlights the problem solving aspect is to try to set the computer to control an external device. Controlling a Meccano motor, setting information from a light source, switching model railway points are ideal problems for pupils to tackle. They are motivating, easily achieved and have a fascinatingly attractive outcome.

(3) It explains about the computer

A third reason for teaching control in Computer Studies is that it directly illustrates what a computer is and how it works. Input, output, process and feedback are visible and not contained in black boxes produced by the manufacturer.

(4) It is technology

Technology is a desperately undervalued subject in schools: "General technology ...must now be regarded as an integral part of any individual's general education for citizenship" [2]. Technology directly teaches skills and concepts that are often used by other subjects to justify their own place on the curriculum but which are usually lost in overcrowded syllabuses and exam techniques. Objectives like teaching the ability to solve problems, the ability to communicate ideas, to research and design often appear on mathematics, science and humanities syllabuses but how often are they implemented? The section on 'Craft, Design and Technology' in the HMI document *Curriculum* 11-16 [3], outlines the objectives for technology teaching. They constitute 'good' education. I believe that technology as a subject would be a better education than the majority of subjects taught in schools now, and should be encouraged to grasp any method of improving its status. Microelectronic control provides this opportunity because it is both creative and exciting.

Fig. 13.2 – Christopher Clayton and David Talbot (5th years) and their computer controlled plotter.

13.3 HOW TO USE THE PET FOR COMPUTER CONTROL

There are two problems involved in using computers to control devices; programming the computer to produce the right signals and interfacing the device to be controlled so that these signals produce the right effect. The PET has various means of connecting to the outside world; the IEEE port, the user port, the cassette port and the extra memory connectors. The main emphasis of the work at the Anthony Gell School has been to investigate how pupils can use the USER port of the PET programmed in BASIC to control equipment like model railways, Meccano motors etc.

Programming the computer

Figure 13.3 represents the way information within the computer can be turned into electrical signals or vice versa. Two memory locations are used, one to switch on and off the signals (59471) and one to control their direction (59459). The PET stores data in memory locations, each location can contain a binary pattern from 00000000 to 11111111. Each memory location or store contains 8 binary digits (bits) which allow eight simultaneous signals to be input or output from the computer.

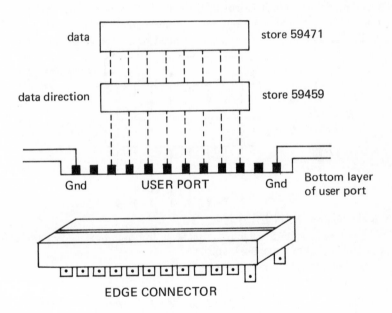

Fig. 13.3 – Conversion of information in the computer into electrical signals (or vice-versa).

Each memory location can be changed by using the POKE command. For example POKE 59471,160 and POKE 59459,63 would give:

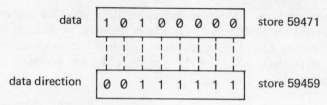

data   1 0 1 0 0 0 0 0   store 59471

data direction   0 0 1 1 1 1 1 1   store 59459

Note that 160 = 10100000   in binary
                 63 = 00111111

To look at the data in any particular memory location the function PEEK is used. For example, if store 59471 contains 10011111 then X = PEEK (59471) will give X the value of 159 since 10011111 in binary equals 159.

Output
The PET has a flexible input/output system and the store 59459 governs the direction of the data. If a bit in 59459 is set to 1 then that line is set for output and the data bit from 59471 is output on the user port as 5 volts or 0 volts depending on whether it is 1 or 0. If the bit in 59459 is 0 then the line is set for input and the bit in 59471 is put equal to the signal from the outside world.

To use all eight bits as output we need to change all of the bits in 59459 to 1:

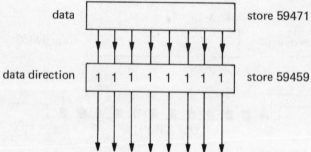

data   store 59471

data direction   1 1 1 1 1 1 1 1   store 59459

This can be done by POKE 59459,255.

When this is done the output pins on the user port reflect the status of store 59471. (1 = 5 volts, 0 = 0 volts.)

For example, POKE 59459,255: POKE 59471,133.

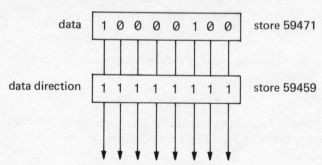

data   1 0 0 0 0 1 0 0   store 59471

data direction   1 1 1 1 1 1 1 1   store 59459

By this means the computer can be programmed to produce 5 or 0 volts at up to 1 m A to any of the middle eight pins on the bottom edge of the user port.

Input
To use all eight bits for input we need to change all of the bits in 59459 to 0:

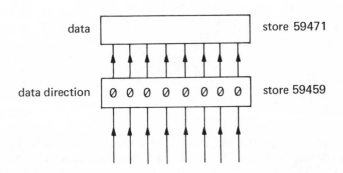

So to change all eight pins to input the command POKE 59459,0 is used.

When this is done the value of 59471 reflects the voltages on the user port pins (1 = 5 volts. 0 = 0 volts).
For example, POKE 59459,255.

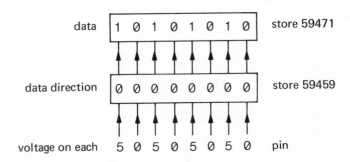

PRINT PEEK (59471) would give 170 (10101010 in binary).

The useful part about input in the PET is that the computer holds the pins at 5v, so that simply by connecting the pins to the ground, inputs can be detected.

Input/Output
Output and input can be mixed of course, either using different pins for each or by changing 59459 during the program.
For example, POKE 59459,240 sets four for output, four for input.

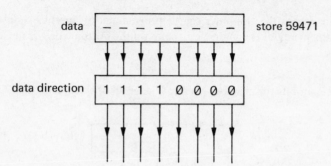

Interfacing the computer

Principles

The user port is a 24 way (0.156 inch edge connector) contact. The 8 pins connected to the locations 59471 and 59459 described above are PA0 to PA7 which are the middle eight connections on the bottom row of the user port. Input is easy to do and our first experiment at school was with a paper clip earthing various of the pins. Try this program:

```
10POKE59459,0
20PRINT PEEK(59471);
30GOTO20
```

You should see:

```
255 255 255 255 255 255 255 255 255
255 255 255 255 255 255 255 255 255
255 255 255 255 255 255 255 255 255
255 255 255 255 etc.
```

If you now take a wire connected to earth (the outside pins on the user port) and touch PA0 to 7 in turn the value should change.

```
255 255 255 254 254 254 255 255 255
253 253 253 255 255 255 255 251 251
251 251 255 255 255 247 247 247 247
247 247 247 247 etc.
```

Notice that for 247 the value has been reduced by 8 which indicates that PA3 has been earthed:

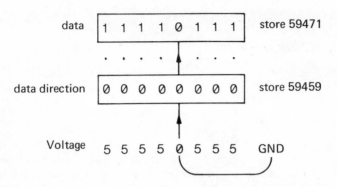

Therefore to interface for input all you need is a suitable connector and a means of connecting to earth. It is possible to use opto-isolators to isolate your computer from any possible damage but because the PET can use ground signals only for input it is easy to ensure safe operation.

To interface for output is more complicated because of the low current available (1 mA). This can drive a TTL circuit although we find it more convenient to use the signal to switch the current that can be drained through a Darlington pair. (Fig. 13.4).

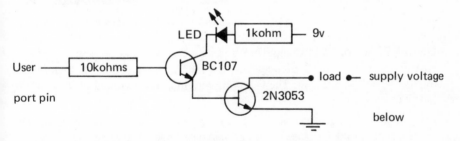

Fig. 13.4 — Darlington pair used to drive loads at up to 1 amp.

We have built interface boxes to house these circuits attached to each of the eight pins. The following is a description of such an interface box designed and built by Michael Hooton (5th year).

Interface Box
The PET Interface Box (Fig. 13.5) allows electrical devices to be connected to the PET directly. It enables lamps, motors, relays, switches, etc. to be controlled by the PET. Full control of motors is also provided (On/Off, Reverse). The unit also provides a sound output from the CB2 pin on the PET. It is mainly designed for use in schools where a robust unit is needed that plugs straight into the PET and connects directly to motors, lamps, etc. It would be a useful device in

Fig. 13.5 — Michael Hooton and Sheila Parry with Interface box.

Control Technology and Computer Studies courses. The unit plugs into the User Port at the rear of the PET, and also into the mains supply. It is then ready for use when switched on. The following terminals are provided on the top of the box:

(a) 8 Input terminals for connecting sensing devices such as switches. Each one protects the PET against common mistakes made when attaching devices to the User Port.

(b) 8 Output terminals for driving motors, lamps, etc., up to 1 Amp maximum current.

(c) CB2 terminal for handshaking or producing sound.

(d) SPK terminal for inputting signals to the internal audio amplifier. Pins CB2 and SPK should be connected to produce normal sound from the PET. Other sound sources can be connected to the SPK terminal and the internal amplifier used to listen to the signal. The amplifier also has a volume control.

(e) +5V and +12V terminals providing power to drive projects such as small robots, cranes, etc.

(f) GND terminal as universal ground connection.

Each of the 8 inputs/outputs has an LED which indicates the state of each input/output.

These boxes are in continual use in the school for various projects (Fig. 13.6) and the technical specifications in Appendix 1 might help other people to build their own, although commercial systems are coming onto the market.

Fig. 13.6 – Richard Weywell – Robot with Interface Box.

13.4 PUPIL PROJECTS

Computing is a relatively new and exciting subject in schools. Previous educational technology has never fulfilled its claim for being an invaluable aid to the teacher. Many enthusiastic teachers do make use of various devices but learning today is still essentially done through personal contact and the written word.

One could argue that teachers are basically conservative and tend to ignore innovation by using the following argument: "I have only got time to teach the essentials. A topic is only essential if it is on the exam syllabus. If it is on the exam syllabus it can be easily taught without recourse to fancy gadgets otherwise schools without them would be penalised. Since I can teach to the exam syllabus by pencil and paper, and since all new gadgets require time and effort then I am having nothing to do with computers".

Although the exam syllabus cannot be ignored teachers must realise that a microcomputer is a device which enables education to happen in its widest sense. It allows realistic open ended problems to be set. The microcomputer in a school can produce considerable motivation and concentration in pupils otherwise bored by learning; more importantly it indicates that education needs to change its emphasis.

Teachers and pupils will have to come to terms with a future society based on microelectronics and information technology. No longer will the remembering of facts be important. No longer will knowledge be static. The people who will do best in a microelectronic society will be the ones who can be flexible, solve problems, work with others, learn new skills, etc. Although significant changes have occurred in our education system we are still dominated by the view that school is concerned with the expert teacher imparting their wisdom to the novice pupil.

I believe we must change from this approach. Teachers sometimes have to take on the role of enablers. They must enable pupils to learn skills and expertise by providing the resources and the motivation but avoid the trap of always wanting to be the expert in command. Microcomputers provide an excellent opportunity to encourage independent thinking and learning. Anyone who has been in schools knows that the real expertise lies with the pupils. Teachers have to accept this fact and be glad of it. Rather than try and turn computer education into a dry academic subject we must keep up this excitement and interest. To do this I believe we must give our pupils open ended projects that require all sorts of skills and which motivate pupils to learn for themselves. The following are accounts of some of the projects worked on at Anthony Gell.

A coin input keyboard

An interesting and easy area for pupils to start investigating is the building of other keyboards to operate the computer. Because these keyboards can rely solely on earth inputs they are safe for those not wanting to endanger their computer with input voltages. The following project on a coin input box was started by a fourth year pupil, Nicholas Howard. Very often simple remedial programs require money input and it seemed a good idea to use the coins for the buttons themselves. After seeing a similar keyboard for the Tandy devised in Walsall we decided that it would be useful to build our own. The idea is that if someone presses the 10p coin it goes into the computer as 10p. The pupil can then ignore the computer keyboard entirely and concentrate on a simple box with the coins as shown in Fig. 13.7.

This has obvious applications to remedial and special education.

Construction

The PET is ideally suited for keyboards of this kind if they are connected via the User port. This takes input as an earth signal so that there is no need to generate voltages. The construction of the keyboard is shown in Appendix 2.

Fig. 13.7 – Nicholas Howard with coin-input keyboard.

Programming

Again the PET is easy to use for input via the User port. The following subroutine puts X equal to the value in pence of the key pressed. It returns -1 if the return key is pressed.

```
2000 REM SUBROUTINE TO INPUT FROM COIN KEYBOARD
2010 POKE 59459,0 : REM SETS TO INPUT
2020 XX=PEEK(59471) : REM GETS VALUE
2030 IF XX=255THEN2020 : REM NO INPUT
2040 IF XX=254THENX=.5 : REM 1/2P
2050 IF XX=253THENX=1 : REM 1P
2060 IF XX=251THENX=2 : REM 2P
2070 IF XX=247THENX=5 : REM 5P
2080 IF XX=239THENX=10 : REM 10P
2090 IF XX=223THENX=50 : REM 50P
2100 IF XX=191THENX=-1 : REM RETURN
2110 FORDD=1TO150 : NEXT : REM PREVENTS KEY BOUNCE
2200 RETURN
```

Notice that the normal return from a PEEK (59471) is 255 since the inputs are kept at 1 until grounded by the key press.

A simple program incorporating the subroutine above would be:

```
10 REM MONEY SUM
30 REM 26/1/81
100C=10
110V1=INT(RND(1)*C):V2=INT(RND(1)*C+5)
120PRINT"CALCULATE THE VALUE OF "V1 "+" V2 "=?PENCE"
130PRINT"PRESS THE COINS TO THIS VALUE UNTIL THEY"
140PRINT"ADD UP TO THE ANSWER-THEN PRESS THE"
150PRINT"END BUTTON"
160TT=0
170GOSUB2000:IF X=-1THEN200
180PRINT X"+";
190TT=TT+X:GOTO170
200IF TT⟨⟩(V1+V2)THENPRINT"HARD LUCK TRY AGAIN":GOTO120
210PRINT"WELL DONE":C=C+1:GOTO110
```

Obviously this is a fairly limited program but gives the idea of what can be done.

So far we have used the keyboard successfully with remedial pupils. We have built and sent a coin input keyboard to a school for the physically handicapped who have sent word that it is providing useful experience for their pupils.

A simple robot
by Catherine Howard (6th Form)
The reason for the school having PETs is that they can be used to control external equipment very easily. One of the first projects we started was a very simple robot (Fig. 13.8). The very first robot we made is able to move forwards and sideways but not backwards. What follows is about this first attempt at robotics and a few notes on subsequent improvements.

Construction
The robot itself was a simple Meccano chasis with two Meccano motors mounted on it. Wires are taken from the motors through a long lead to the interface box that we have designed (see Appendix 3).

Programming
The first program written for this robot was the one listed below:

```
5PRINT"clear screen"
10PRINT"PRESS 4 FOR LEFT"
12PRINT"        6 FOR RIGHT"
14PRINT"        8 FOR FORWARD"
16PRINT"        S FOR STOP"
20POKE 59459,255
30P=32928:Q=32968:R=33008:C=59471
```

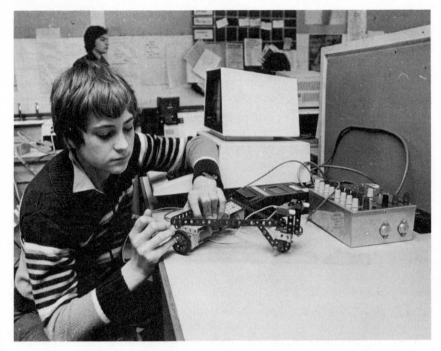

Fig. 13.8 – Richard Brewell (2nd year) building his own robot.

40IF PEEK(151)=42THEN POKEC,128 : A=60 : GOSUB100
50IF PEEK(151)=50THEN POKEC,192 : A=30 : GOSUB100
60IF PEEK(151)=41THEN POKEC,64 : A=62 : GOSUB100
70IF PEEK(151)=40THEN POKEC,0 : POKE158,0 : END
80IF PEEK(151)=255THEN POKEC,0 : A=32 : GOSUB100
90GOTO40
100FORI=5TO8 : POKEP+I,A : POKEQ+I,A : POKER+I,A : NEXTI
110RETURN

NOTE – If your PET has old ROMs then 151 should be 515 and 518 should
be 525.

Explanation of program
    Lines 5 to 16 clear the screen and give instructions.
    Line 20 sets all the pins on the User port to output. (255 is 11111111
in binary. 1 indicates to the computer to output a signal; each bit is said to be
high.)
    Line 30 sets the variables P,Q,R, and C. P,Q,R are memory locations; when
values are put into memory locations 32768 to 33767 a character is displayed on

the screen in the appropriate position, the poke code of this character corresponds to the value in the store. C is the number of the memory location for the output of data to the User port.

In lines 40-60 the computer 'looks' at store 151. This store holds the keyboard code for the key which is being pressed. The keyboard codes for 4,5,6 are 41,34,42; if 4 is being pressed peek (151) = 41, the computer will do nothing on line 40 or 50 but on line 60 the computer will put 64 into store 59471 (C). 64 is 01000000 in binary so only one output pin will be high (only one signal is sent out) and this signal goes through the interface box to drive the right motor so turning the robot to the left. If 5 is pressed both motors are operated, if 6 is pressed the left motor runs.

Line 70 stops the robot. 40 is the keyboard code for 'S' and if this is pressed 59471 is set to zero. No signals are output and the robot stops. Location 158 (or 525 on old PETs) is the place which counts the number of key presses and at the end of the program the stored characters are printed out. To avoid this POKE 158, 0; the computer then 'thinks' there are no characters stored. (Store 158 counts is what is called a buffer, each new symbol shunts the others along until the tenth character is discarded.)

Line 80. If no key is being pressed the value in memory location 151 is 255. If the computer finds this value in this location it stops all signals to the robot. This means that the robot will only move while a key is being pressed. If this line is not included once a key has been pressed the robot will continue and only stop when 'S' is pressed.

Line 90 just gets the computer to start the checking process all over again.

Line 100. On lines 40-80 a value of A has been set and the computer shows on the screen the direction the robot is moving by a set of arrows.

Computer controlled model railway

In this project the PET microcomputer was used to control a simple railway system (Fig. 13.9). The students involved were a group of fourth year boys including Karl Else, Neil Davies, David Talbot and several others. Richard Waymell, Michael Hooton and Simeon Jones also became involved from time to time.

The track layout is shown in Fig. 13.10. It consists of a simple loop with various sidings. The power is fed to the rails and the points from the interface box. The train is detected by three detectors as shown on the diagram. These consist of reed switches, whose contacts are made by the passage of a truck fitted with a small magnet underneath. Before going into the technical details of how the pupils built the equipment I will describe the general running of the program.

When the program is loaded and run the user is given a menu of possible uses:

DIRECT MODE

RECORD MODE
EXECUTE MODE
SAVE MODE
CALL MODE

The DIRECT MODE takes the train on the track to its starting point (labelled S on the diagram). It then displays a map of the track on the screen and gives the user a choice so that they are in control of the track directly from the keyboard. The five possible choices are:

(1) Track current ON/OFF. This supplies the power to the train depending on the conditions set by 2 and 5.
(2) FORWARD/REVERSE. This changes the direction of the train.
(3) Quit to Menu. Returns to start.

Fig. 13.9 – Karl Else with computer controlled model railway.

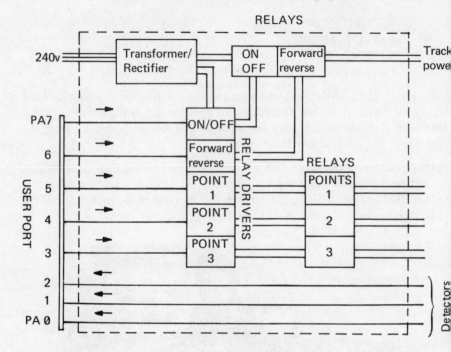

Track diagram

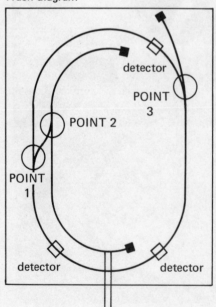

Fig. 13.10 – Railway Interface Box diagram and Track layout.

(4) Operate point – it then requests number of the point to switch.
(5) Slow speed ON/OFF. This pulses the voltage supply so that a slower train speed is obtained.

The computer is therefore acting as a super train controller. It is not until the RECORD, SAVE and EXECUTE modes are used that the computer comes into its own:

RECORD MODE. In this mode the same functions are available as the DIRECT MODE but the computer remembers the key presses and their timing. The computer is therefore acting as a teachable programmable device very similar to the arc welding and paint spraying robots used on car assembly lines.

SAVE MODE. Having recorded a sequence of events the computer can save it to disk for later recall.

CALL MODE. To retrieve a sequence from disk so that it can be executed.

EXECUTE MODE. The computer returns the train to its start position and runs through the sequence stored in memory. This is reasonably accurate although it is advisable not to stop the train too close to the points when they change!

This gives some idea of the project so far. Obviously it is possible to extend it indefinitely in size and sophistication but it represents a significant achievement on the part of a group of fourteen year olds with under a year's computer experience.

PROGRAM DESCRIPTION

The PET is relatively easy to program for control purposes through the user port. This has eight contacts whose state reflect the binary number of a memory location. These can be programmed for input and output. In fact three of them act as inputs from the reed switches, two are outputs for the track voltage and three are used to switch the points. Apart from a machine code subroutine the program was written entirely in BASIC.

INTERFACE DESCRIPTION

The interface box consists of a transformer to supply the power, several relay drivers to boost up the signal from the PET to switch a relay, and several capacitors to provide a surge of current to switch the points. The technical details are published elsewhere [4].

The project has been extremely successful: it has achieved its aims. This has not been due to my help as their teacher since most of the knowledge, initiative and effort has come from the pupils. It represents an ideal demonstration of the way computers can be used for control. It is one of many projects that pupils are undertaking at the school to use the computer for simple control purposes. I think it is important to do this kind of work if what we teach in schools is going to provide the type of expertise to make the best use of microelectronics.

Computer controlled model house
Michael Hooton and Catherine Howard.

The starting point for this project was the need to find a method of testing effective ways to conserve energy. We thought that a lot of energy could be saved if buildings were properly insulated. In order to find out the relative effectiveness of different insulators and energy saving ideas we have built a computer controlled and monitored model house (Fig. 13.11).

Fig. 13.11 – Michael and Catherine with the house.

CONSTRUCTION

The model itself is constructed mainly from hardboard panels. There is a hardboard base mounted on soft roofing board. The walls are bolted onto wooden batons which are in turn glued and screwed to the base. The outer walls have a cavity between them and the inner partitions are single pieces of hardboard. All the walls are totally detatchable, the roof is also made of hardboard and is sloping.

Within the house we have used bulbs to represent radiators, people, a cooker and a fire. These are all wired up with ribbon cable and are connected via an interface box to the user port of the PET. The bulbs can be controlled directly by the use of the keyboard or a sequence of instructions can be inputted and stored to be run at any time. Before a sequence is run you must specify how long each simulated minute should last, each minute can last a full sixty seconds down to a fraction of a second. This enables us to simulate a complete day in any particular time that is convenient to the experiment. The sequence can be stored on a disk, tape or even be printed out. By using a sequence we are able to do exactly the same experiment time and time again with complete accuracy.

Displayed on the PET's screen is a plan of the house (Fig. 13.12) and an indication of which bulbs are on. If a sequence is being run the next operation is shown and a bleep produced, via the loud speaker in the interface box, as each instruction is carried out.

We use another PET to monitor the system. In each room there is a thermistor which records the temperature, there are also two thermistors outside the model. The wires from the thermistor are fed through an analog to digital converter into the user and IEEE ports of the second PET. The average outside temperature is calculated, adjustments being made to compensate for differences between each thermistor. The difference between the average outside temperature and the temperature within each room is displayed on a plan view of the house on the screen in the appropriate place.

If necessary the temperatures can be stored on disk or tape. If a sequence is over, say, twelve hours (thirty seconds for every 'minute') the temperatures are stored in the computer's memory and are transferred to disk or printer at the end of the experiment. The information can be printed out as either a table of the individual temperatures in each room and outside or as separate graphs of the temperature variation in each individual room.

Using this system it is easy to make comparisons between different types of insulators. Weather factors are eliminated, the same test is run every time and the results are recorded automatically. Being on a small scale insulators can be quickly and easily changed. As we built a model house rather than testing the insulators directly, by testing the amount of heat to pass through a certain insulator in a certain time, we are able to test to discover how useful it would be to use a certain colour on the outer walls or if a sloping roof is worse, from an energy saving point of view than a flat roof. We are not able to say that if our results were scaled up a certain amount of heat would be lost, but we are able to make comparisons between different energy saving ideas.

With the software and interfacing system we have produced we could monitor a full scale house by just wiring up the sensors and recording the temperture fluctuations. By using two PETs, one to drive the house and one to monitor, it would be difficult to keep the house at a given temperature. This, however, would not be too difficult if we used a single PET but we did not for ease of programming. At the moment we know the temperature at any given time and with only slight modification we could get the computer to produce a suitable signal to the bulbs depending on this temperature. The problem is that there are only 8 pins for both input and output so we would have had to cut down on the number of independent bulbs and the number of thermistors. We all found that we learned a lot from doing the project and hope we will able to get some results from it.

PLAN OF HOUSE

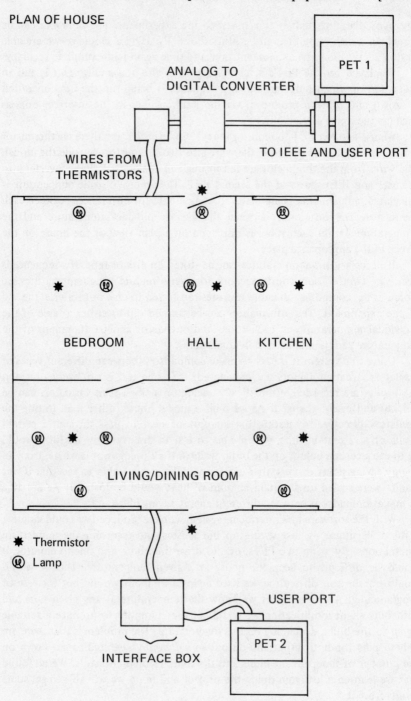

Fig. 13.12 – Plan of Model House.

KIM controlled robot

The idea of a robot has a endless fascination and with the involvement of micro-electronic technology has important commercial and industrial applications. Since schools have an involvement in teaching people for a future society it is important that they develop an awareness of the possibilities in this field. One excellent way of doing this is to get pupils to produce their own simple robots. Below is a description by Michael Hooton, a fifth year pupil, of a simple KIM controlled robot (Fig. 13.13) which is able to find its own way around and to 'intelligently' avoid obstacles.

It is an experimental design which consists of a Meccano chassis supporting a single board microcomputer called the KIM. The chassis has two motors to allow it to move around, and two sensing switches at the front to detect if it hits anything.

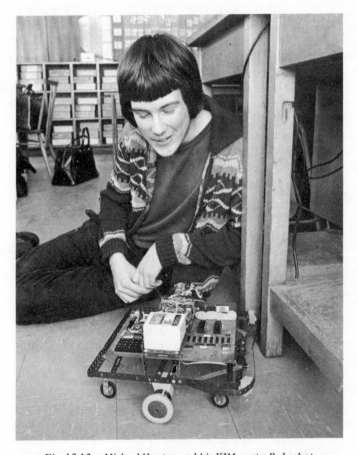

Fig. 13.13 – Michael Hooton and his KIM controlled robot.

This robot has the major advantage over many others in that it is completely self contained. No wires dangle from the robot to connect it to a source of power and a computer, which will limit its range and freedom. The computer and the power source are both mounted on the robot. This robot can be used to experiment with path-finding techniques, and how to get through a maze. At the start, however, the robot will simply be programmed to avoid obstacles.

The robot is constructed from Meccano in a square shape. The two Meccano motors are mounted underneath, about halfway along opposite sides. The sensing switches are very sensitive (or low torque) microswitches, which are mounted at the front corners of the robot. Each switch has a wire lever protruding from it which stick out in front. A light wooden bar or rod was fastened between these two wires. If an object is encountered in front of the robot then it will push the bar back into the robot and trigger the switches.

The KIM microcomputer board takes up about two thirds of the top of the square. The remaining third is used to mount the electronics. A gantry was built over the top of the computer to carry the batteries. Onto the front and back of the frame were mounted four stabilizing wheels.

The power for the robot comes from two main batteries. Both of these are Nickel Cadmium rechargeable types to provide the high currents needed. One of these batteries is 8.4v at 1.2Ah and powers the relays and KIM. The KIM needs 5V and so the supply is regulated. The other consists of four 1.25V batteries to power the motors.

The sensing switches are connected directly between the KIMs inputs and ground. Normally the KIM holds the input at logic 1 but when an object switches a microswitch this sets a bit to logic 0. The state of the switches can therefore be read by looking at the status of the input/output register of the KIM.

The outputs of the KIM provide only a few mA of current. To drive the motors the outputs are fed into transistor amplifiers which operate relays. This isolates the motors from the KIM an also allows reverse movements.

The program (Appendix 4) was put onto EPROM to avoid reloading each time.

Using the Commodore PET's Assembler a program was written so that the robot avoided obstacles. If both switches are hit at the same time then the robot reverses and turns through $90°$ to avoid the obstacle. If only one switch is activated then the robot reverses and turns through $45°$ away from the obstacle. If the same event happens three times then the robot assumes that it has got stuck in a corner and reverses and then turns through 180 degrees.

PET MAS

As a by-product of our work on control applications we have developed a multiple access system. Like many of the developments this was produced by Michael Hooton in his fifth year at school. The PET Multiple Access System or PetMas allows up to 7 PET computers to access common IEEE devices such as the disk drive and printer. This system is a cheap method of allowing several computers to have immediate access to disk files and a hard copy facility, as the master and slave units cost us about £25 each to manufacture.

The system consists of a central control box which connects to the disk/ printer, and also plugs into the mains, providing power to the whole system. A separate 'slave' unit is then required for each PET in the system (up to 7), which plugs into the back of the PET. Each unit provides a connecting cable with plug which plugs into the previous unit, the last one in the chain plugs into the control unit. Everything is then switched on and the system is ready to use.

Only one PET can have access at any one time. If a PET already has access any other PETs wanting access are held by the system until the first PET has finished and then they are given access.

The control unit has a display indicating when the system is switched on, and which PET is accessing at any time. A switch on the control unit allows access to be denied to everybody while disks or printer paper are being changed. The switch also allows just one PET to have complete access without any interference from other users, useful for many file handling programs.

A special unit is also available allowing local devices to be connected to certain PETs. With this unit a PET can have a printer connected to do a lot of printing without 'hogging' the main system for long periods. The device can be switched between allowing access to the local device or the main system. The switching can be done manually with a switch or automatically within a program. Some word processor programs allow control of this facility, enabling the program to fetch files off the central disk, switch to the local printer, and print them out. The program can be left to do this on its own for several files; only interfering with the main system when a file is required off disk. We hope to get a commercial manufacturer interested in this since it is much cheaper than the available hardware rivals and more adaptable than software versions.

REFERENCES

[1] *Syllabus for the future*, Schools committee working party of the BCS.
[2] Standing Conference of European Ministers of Education, 1978.
[3] *DES Curriculum*, 11-16, HMSO.
[4] *Computer Education*, June 1981.
[5] *Compute In Schools*, July 1981.
[6] *The PET Revealed*, N. Hampshire.

Acknowledgements
To Computers In Schools for permission to duplicate illustrations, the Department of Trade and Industry for financial support and Derbyshire LEA for financial and other support.

Part (a) of Appendix 1 – The interface box-interface unit for PET computer.

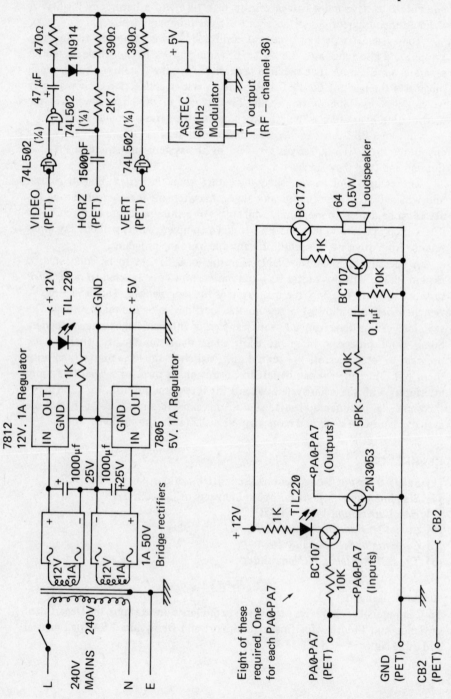

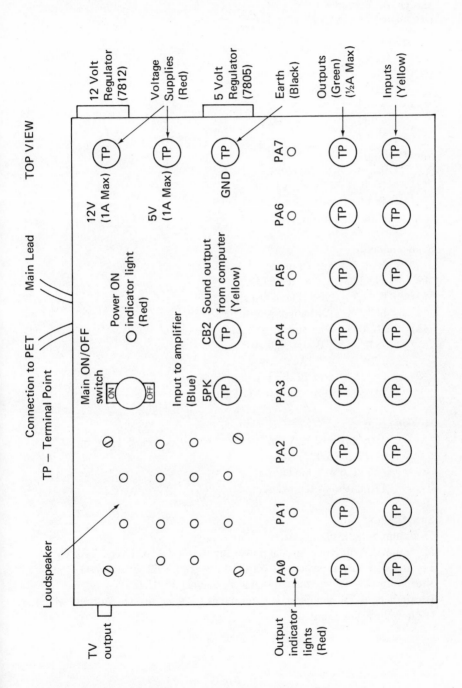

Part (b) of Appendix 1
COMPONENT LIST

Resistors

(10)	10K	
(10)	1K	
	2K7	¼W ± 5%
(2)	390Ω	
	470Ω	

Capacitors

	0.1 µF	Disc ceremic
(2)	1000 µF	25V electrolyte
	47 µF	electrolytic
	1500 pF	Polystyrene

Semiconductors

	1N914	Silicon diode
(9)	TlL220	0.2 in Red LED
(9)	BC107	NPN silicon transistor
	BC177	PNP silicon transistor
(8)	2N3053	NPN silicon transistor
	7812	12V 1A regulator
	7805	5V 1A regulator
	1A	50V Bridge rectifier
	74LS02	Quad 2-input NOR gate

Miscellaneous

250V primary; 12V 1A, 12V 1A secondary, transformer
64Ω 0.5W loudspeaker
ASTEC 6MHz modulator
Terminals, switch, wire, etc.

Specifications

Maximum output sinking current − 500mA
Maximum current from internal power supplies − 1A for 12V, 1A for 5V
Loudspeaker output power − 2 Watts (drives from CB2 squarewave)
Video output − RF modulated signal on channel 36 (UHF)
Isolation between computer and terminals − None, except outputs which are isolated through a transistor

Appendix 2 – Construction of coin-input keyboard.

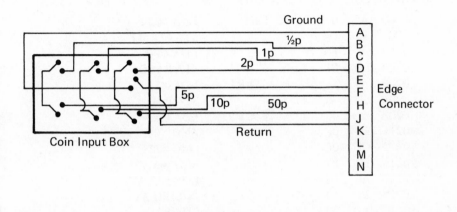

Ground

½p

1p

2p

5p

10p   50p

Return

Coin Input Box

A
B
C
D
E
F
H
J
K
L
M
N

Edge
Connector

Appendix 3 – Construction plan of robot.

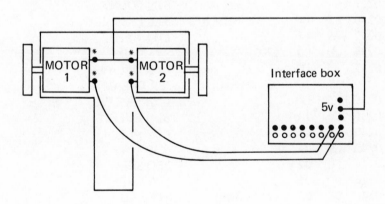

MOTOR
1

MOTOR
2

Interface box

5v

Appendix 4

MACHINE CODE FOR KIM ROBOT

0200	A9	03		INIT	LDA #03
0202	85	D4			STA COUNT
0204	A9	F0			LDA #F0
0206	8D	01	17		STA PADD
0209	A9	5F		START	LDA #5F
020B	8D	00	17		STA PAD
020E	AD	00	17	WAIT	LDA PAD
0211	29	0C			AND #0C
0213	CD	0C			CMP #0P
0215	F0	F7			BEQ WAIT
0217	A6	D1			LDX DELAY1
0219	20	10	03		JSR DELAY
021C	AD	00	17		LDA PAD
021F	29	0C			AND #0C
0221	C5	D0			CMP LASMVE
0223	D0	07			BNE NESCAP1
0225	C6	D4			DEC COUNT
0227	D0	07			BNE NESCAP2
0229	4C	60	02		JMP ROTATE
022C	A0	03		NESCAP1	LDY #03
022E	84	D4			STY COUNT
0230	85	D0		NESCAP2	STA LASMVE
0232	A9	FF			LDA #FF
0234	8D	00	17		STA PAD
0237	A6	D2			LDX DELAY2
0239	20	10	03		JSR DELAY
023C	A5	D0			LDA LASMVE
023E	F0	13			BEQ FULHIT
0240	AQ	CF			LDY #CF
0242	C9	04			CMP #04
0244	F0	02			BEQ SKIP
0246	A0	3F			LDY #3F
0248	8C	00	17	SKIP	STY PAD
024B	A6	D3			LDX DELAY3
024D	20	10	03		JSR DELAY
0250	4C	09	02		JMP START
0253	AQ	7F		FULHIT	LDY #7F
0255	8C	00	17		STY PAD
0258	A6	D5			LDX DELAY4
025A	20	10	03		JSR DELAY

```
025D   4C   09   02              JSR START
0260   A9   FF          ROTATE   LDA #FF
0262   8D   00   17              STA PAD
0265   A6   D2                   LDX DELAY2
0267   20   10   03              JSR DELAY
026A   A9   DF                   LDA #DF
026C   8D   00   17              STA PAD
026F   A6   D6                   LDX DELAY5
0271   20   10   03              JSR DELAY
0274   4C   00   02              JMP INIT

0300   48                INRPT   PHA
0301   A9   0F                   LDA #0F
0303   8D   00   17              STA PAD
0306   68                        PLA
0307   4C   00   1C              JUMP 1C00
0310   A9   28          DELAY    LDA #28
0312   8D   07   17              STA 1707
0315   2C   07   17     LOOP     BIT 1707
0318   10   F8                   BPL LOOP
031A   CA                        DEX
031B   D0   F3                   BNE DELAY
031D   60                        RTS
```

CHAPTER 14

PETS in the practical class: the case for computer assisted experimentation

Christopher Smith, Queen Elizabeth College, University of London, London

---

Much of the delight that children, and others, have in using computers is that computers do things. The screens dance with images of spaceships; printers tell the distance to touch-down. So why not let the computer do things for real?

This article describes the way that microcomputers can be treated as part of the apparatus for real experiments and how this allows computer hardware and software to be seen in the setting of a particular subject rather than in terms of computer science.

14.1 DIFFERING ROLES FOR THE USE OF MICROCOMPUTER IN EDUCATION

A schism in computer-assisted learning

Even a brief inspection of programs used in education shows two separate design philosophies. One, which may be defined as the intelligent book format, sets out to provide facts and ideas in a way commensurate with the students' responses. The second, experiment simulation, provides data from a model in accord with the students' manipulation of the model. Whilst all computer programs are in essence a model, the second type is distinguished by the model being the subject of study rather than a means to an end. In the intelligent book format the computer is seen as a device for manipulating language; in the simulation of experiments the computer is considered as a device for calculating responses.

Surprisingly the nomenclature of these types of programs is not clear. Many people would accept CAI (computer-aided instruction) as a term to describe programs that manipulate language. CAL (computer-assisted learning) is a term often used by users of simulation programs but is clearly a very broad term. In this paper I will refer to these types of program as CAS – computer-assisted simulation.

Computer-assisted simulation

CAS has proven to be a most successful use of microcomputers in schools. It has two important practical advantages: the format of CAS fits easily into the school's teaching schedule — that is, as an 'experiment' in the laboratory classes. Secondly the relative compactness of its algorithmic solutions suits well the limited capacity of low-priced microcomputer systems.

These advantages are complemented by advances in the art of CAS promoted by the use of microcomputers. These mainly derive from the ability of the program to control the operating system, in particular the keyboard input and video display routines, which allow a remarkably fluid display and control of the simulation: compare, for example, current moonlander programs with those derived from scrolled terminal versions.

The design of screen displays for CAS is complex. The problem is that three logically separate components need to be shown; the actual data produced by the simulation, the variables for the control of the experiment and those for the control of the program sequence. Watching students' responses to CAS quickly shows how easy it is to become confused between these components. It is analogous to the common problem where, perhaps due to the lack of fool-proof programming, the student is confused between computer operating system messages and program messages.

One solution developed at Chelsea is to physically separate the logical components on to different areas of the video screen. The advent of relatively cheap colour graphics is of particular value here to provide different background hues to the logical sections. However, even with these programs it has proved tempting to define an 'input' screen region — rather than keeping each input within its own logical region. One reason for this is the limited screen resolution once the screen has been subdivided into regions.

A second approach, in recognition of the intention to simulate an experiment as closely as possible, is to direct data input and output away from the screen to some other physical device. At the simple level an example would be in the teaching of Ohm's law of resistance; the output current or voltage of a simulation can easily and cheaply be directed via a digital to analog converter to a voltmeter. A second stage would be to add an analog converter to monitor the performance of a real resistor. The CAL program could then direct and check the student's experiment.

At this stage it is of course clear that we no longer have a simulation but a real live experiment for use in education. Yet another acronym seems called for: CAE — computer assisted experimentation.

The case for computer assisted experimentation (CAE)

It is perhaps axiomatic that a real experiment is preferable to its simulation and thus that the argument for CAE should be reversed; when should one simulate an experiment rather than actually do it? There are two types of answer: when it cannot be done and when it is just inconvenient. Impossibility comes from the time-scale, such as in genetics, from the physical scale as in a study of ocean currents and from the inherent danger of some experiments. The inconvenience of CAL lies substantially in the assumption of it needing expensive, complex and little-understood equipment. Whilst in the past this may have been true, transducers and computer interfaces have, like computers, become more accessible in both price and ease of use. Indeed the provision of analogue interfacing within the designs of two recent microcomputers, the Newbrain and the Proton, makes it clear that CAE is here to stay.

Examples from my particular educational interest concern tertiary level teaching about the human cardiovascular system. In practice I use both CAS and CAE in the same practical class to illustrate different aspects. Two simulation programs have been in use for several years: MACMAN, the progenitor of a highly detailed set of programs originally developed for teaching medical students at McMaster University but now used even in intensive-care wards to check clinicians' hypotheses, and CIRC, produced during the CUSC (computers in undergraduate science curriculum) project at Chelsea College, London. Both these are now available in microcomputer versions, though only slightly changed from a scrolled screen ('Teletype') format. The former gives a semi-graphical scrolled chart display, the latter gives tabular displays from which comparative graphs may be constructed. Both essentially produce steady-state solutions to algorithms for cardiac contractility, blood distribution and blood vessel dynamics. MACMAN, giving solutions for 4 second iterative steps, shows a ballistic steady state. The programs are used in the teaching class to show the simplicity of an analytical 'Ohm's Law' approach to the circulation and the complexity derived from having two or more interacting control systems.

In contrast, two programs I have developed for use at Queen Elizabeth College concern respectively the collection of real cardiovascular data and the algorithmic generation of cardiovascular 'recordings'. PULSE uses a normal physiological class apparatus to measure in real-time the student's heart beat and lung size. Graphical display of this data on the PET screen leads directly in the classroom to new hypotheses and experimentation. In essence this is a computer-assisted experiment – though the program is written for teaching purposes rather than research. Its role is firmly experimentation, not simulation.

HEARTBEAT is an algorithmic program similar to CIRC but with (a) two-channel analog output and (b) an iterative solution to the aortic (arterial) blood pressure waves during each heartbeat. In initial versions of the program the pulse pressure wave form was the only analog output. However, visual interpretation was greatly improved by including the heart volume as a second output. This effectively replicates the pioneering measurements made by the physiologist, E. H. Starling. The output voltages are recorded on paper chart recorders as in normal student experiments. Interruption of the program by the student to reset variables or to request further data ('clinical tests') shows as a gap on the chart record of the experiment — thus allowing a clearer interpretation of the sequence of program events.

14.2 A HISTORY OF COMPUTERS IN THE LABORATORY

Faced with a laboratory stuffed with electrical equipment it suddenly becomes rather hard to define what a computer is. Given that the rather advanced analogue computers of the late 1950s really are computers what, for example, is the status of a single capacitor used in the 1920s to integrate the electrical response from a muscle? There is an input signal, an output and a 'hardwired' program to link the two. In the same way that the old relay-based telephone exchange was used to provide an analogy of the digital computer it is clear that much of the history of the development of scientific techniques is also the early history of computing.

The postwar achievement is thus primarily in the flexibility of programming, partly by the analogue computer but predominately by the digital computer. The surprising consequence is that the development of modern laboratory computing depended on the production of a single circuit element — the analogue to digital converter. In 1960 the A to D converter barely existed; in 1962 a researcher could describe his converter as a facility to 'to fulfill the needs of a large city' but by the mid 1960s no self-respecting research laboratory (which could afford £15,000) was without its laboratory computer, probably Digital's LINC 8 with a multichannel 10 bit A to D, analogue output to an oscilloscope display and dual processor operation.

From 1965 onwards there has been a steady growth of the use of computers in the professional laboratory with the emphasis shifting from data recording and analysis to closed loop operation. The shift reflects the increased reliability of minicomputers: with the data-crunching role there was inevitably some back-up recording system such as FM tape recording; with closed loop systems the operation of the experiment is almost certain to be totally dependent on the computer being alive.

Types of laboratory operation

The variety and complexity of ways in which a computer is used in the laboratory has forced a new language that is worth describing in some detail — not least because the words are now finding use in normal language. Even with the simplest schools computer it is easy to invent short programs that will demonstrate these definitions if the school children are persuaded to act out the role of the external equipment . . . . 'Who wants to be the thermometer and who will be the analog to digital converter'.

Timing is the first essential in laboratory or real life uses. The computer is *on-line* when it is able to receive and dispose of external data as far as the data is provided; if data disposal (*archiving*) or other reasons stop the flow then the operation is *batch mode*. In *real-time* uses the computer must also be able to treat the external events as part of a time sequence so that it could tell, for example, if smoke came before a fire and it could react before the fire spread. In *strict-time* the computer must keep track of not just the sequence but the actual timing of external events.

A second set of definitions concerns *closed-loop* systems, that is, where a computer output affects a computer input. The feedback is *automative* when the link is provided purely by external machinery and *interactive* where feedback is also provided by the operator. Most laboratory experiments are interactive — even if it only means pushing the PANIC button when things go wrong. The direction of feedback is *conventional* where an input to the computer is used to generate an output which will, somehow, affect the input (though in interactive feedback the operator is assumed to be the controller). The direction is *reflexive* where the controller modifies itself rather than simply creating a new output. It is reflexive control at work where, in a well-designed CAL program, a series of student 'failures' results in the selection of a new strategy of presentation.

The microcomputer in the laboratory

Commercial equipment of, for example, Digital and Hewlett Packard, is very expensive in terms of the average microcomputer users' budget. This cost is only partly due to their smaller turnover, it is mainly their emphasis on (a) speed of data acquisition and disposal and (b) the provision of complete systems from, say, frequency analyser to graphical plotters that work without fuss. However in schools (and in a large number of research applications) these requirements are of low priority and amazingly effective laboratory systems can be put together for £200 to £500 including the micro. In my laboratory 8k PETs are used to stimulate and record the electrical and mechanical responses in isolated muscle preparations and to analyse in strict-time the small and noisy 'blips' from spontaneously active nerve endings. These are facilities which would normally be expected to cost £10,000+.

These sorts of applications require a rigorous use of what I can only call a 'micro mind'. Traditionally the aim of a laboratory system is to record and store as much data as possible, with micros (especially if without disc storage) one must aim to extract the required features as soon as possible. It is not, after all, many experiments that contribute more than 2 or 3 numbers to the final research paper.

14.3 EXAMPLES OF COMPUTER ASSISTED EXPERIMENTATION (CAE)

Experiments requiring no external apparatus

The standard microcomputer has as input and output devices the keyboard and screen. Whilst tolerably satisfactory for communicating with people, these devices are almost hopeless for interacting with the rest of the world. The simplest solution is thus to use people, of which schools usually have an abundant supply, as the transducers to the external world. At a minimum one pupil is the output device and one the input. The former reads the screen and, as directed, takes action. The latter estimates or measures the consequence and types this into the keyboard. This sort of technique has both practical advantages (cost, occupying several people per micro, pleasure in role playing) and the educational value of making machine and logic operations explicit and personal.

A simple example, which would quickly show the advantage of proportional control, would be to keep a beaker of water just simmering by adjusting a gas flame. Concepts of *interrupts* and of *polling* can be introduced by having several 'transducer people' (is gas lit, is there still water in the beaker, is it boiling hard) and even several output people to operate (literal) handshakes.

Perhaps a more popular example would be in describing the problems in operating a robot. The 'robot' should be equipped with flexible antennae so that other people can report collisions to the computer. An alternative is an action program, such as for putting up a fence around a field, which is described (for other reasons) in Chapter 8 of this book.

In most cases the actual computer program used can be simple enough to be written directly by the teacher and pupils. There is however one design feature which must be considered carefully. The screen is going to have on it several different *types* of message, at minimum the 'output' messages and advice and 'input' lines for the keyboard operator. It is recommended that a firm policy is adopted on the physical screen location, preferably enclosed by display boxes, of these types of message. Traditionally (and to match the 380Z) the input prompt and messages come at the bottom of the screen. It is thus worth setting up general cursor control routines for block erasure etc.

Simple laboratory apparatus

The central part of most laboratory computer systems is in effect an intelligent digital storage oscilloscope. With this you can record, display and output analog data; take averages of successive records; smooth data; measure up records and even generate data. Amazingly the PET can be made into such a machine for about £20 and about as many soldering connections. An analog-to-digital converter chip can be wired directly to a user port socket using the CB2 as an output flag to initiate the conversion. Likewise a digital-to-analog chip can be connected to the data lines of the IEEE port (output to which is by a POKE to 59426). Connect up power (from cassette port if a unipolar A-to-D is used, otherwise from the internal main bus) and the analog lines (usually 1 to 2 volt signals) and it is finished. The display can either be on the PET screen (with a vertical resolution using 25 lines and eights symbols of 200 points) or, if available, on to a standard oscilloscope. Good oscilloscope displays are obtained with an array of 256 points. Using BASIC an output sweep takes 1 to 2 seconds; rather more satisfactory is a machine code patch to output a block in less than 10 ms.

Mechanical outputs are usually obtained by turning on and off a D.C. motor. The ideal device would probably be a stepping motor but these are expensive, complex to control and need elaborate power supplies. However in most cases, especially where positioning is required, the best and easiest solution will be to use the actuators designed for the hobby radio-control market. These are now quite cheap (£10) and need only a crude 5v power supply and a logic pulse to control the position. The actuators contain a complete servo-system with the position controlled by the width of the logic pulse, the range being from 1 ms to 2 ms for the extreme positions. The frequency of pulses should be in the range 5 to 100 per second. These sort of devices are ideal for robot arms (typically needing at least four movements) as only one logic line is used for a complete position control. A machine code patch is needed to produce the variable-width pulse.

The simplest mechanical input to a user port is by direct connection of a microswitch (see previous chapter). If an optical switch is needed, for example as a drop-counter to measure liquid flow or for velocity measurement, a device with a built-in amplifier and trigger (for example, Radiospares 304–560) should be used; it eases wiring and operation and costs almost no more than a plain bulb and photodetector. Likewise Radiospares produce a seven channel Darlington driver chip (307–109) which can be used to drive relays etc. from the user port logic signals.

Experiments where the microcomputer is a measuring tool.
The slotted optical switch can be used for both timing and counting, giving immediate access to a wide variety of experiments. Drop counting can be used to measure liquid flow rates such as in viscosity measurements. The laws of motion can be studied by the movement of ball bearings in a perspex guide; assuming that acceleration is to be measured there will need to be three optical switches.

If analog-to-digital converters are not available many measurements can still be made by connecting a sensing resistor (for example, thermistor for temperature, potentiometer for position) into a multivibrator circuit and using the computer to count the number of pulses per second.

In biological experiments the value of a computer-based experiment is often for slow events. Connecting an optical switch to the activity wheel in a rat cage allows one to study, for example, the effect of dark-light timing on the daily (circadian) activity pattern of the rat.

Experiments where the microcomputer is a control device
Many psychological experiments can be conducted using simply the screen and keyboard. A simple reaction time measurement can be used to compare the delays involved in different types of mental processes (recognition of light flashes, words, reading speeds, context errors etc.). Experiments on the visual

system can be undertaken such as for visual clues for size and depth perception. However experiments on visual sensitivity and tracking performance are difficult as the screen can only be changed at intervals of the screen refresh cycle (17 ms for PET).

Using only external logic signals the main features of control loops can be shown. Favourites are the control of washing machines, traffic lights (using optical or magnetic switches to detect the waiting model cars) and, as described in the previous chapter, model trains and robot systems. With these ideas reflexive feedback can be introduced, for example the traffic lights can be made to respond not just to a waiting car but to adjust its operation according to the preceeding average distribution of cars.

In some biological sciences the application of laboratory computer systems is still so new that a school with a microcomputer-based system can conduct original research. Complex training patterns can be used in the study of insect memory development. Growth patterns of seedlings can be investigated using smoothly varying temperature and light cycles instead of the traditional on-off cycles: what, for instance, is the effect of the phase angle between temperature and light cycles?

It will be found that normal pieces of class apparatus can be lashed together with the micro to provide sophisticated instruments at very low additional cost. For instance an optical switch can be set to read the peak deflection of a pH meter; combined with a motorised pump or a relay-controlled drip-feed you now have an autotitrator — for example to measure seedling CO_2 production.

I hope in this article to have given a flavour of what can be achieved in the laboratory with a little effort and brief applications of the soldering iron. During the next two years there will be several packages appearing for laboratory projects in schools. Nevertheless the obvious should never be forgotten, the purpose of doing experiments is to experiment.

CHAPTER 15

Teaching processor architecture and low level languages at 'A' level using a model computer

Peter Bishop, Logica VTS Limited, 64 Newman Street, London

The teaching of Processor Architecture and Low Level Languages at 'A' level poses considerable difficulties. These include lack of training and experience of staff, lack of suitable computing facilities and in particular the absence of a suitable low level programming language to use. There have been numerous attempts to develop low level programming languages in the past [1] but none of these have been particularly successful.

This paper outlines an approach to the topic by the careful design of a model computer (named the AMC) and associated machine and assembly languages, plus a software simulation system which enables students to get 'hands on' experience in this area. It outlines the influences on the design of the system, briefly states the design principles of the machine and the languages, provides an example of an AMC Assembly Language program and discusses the facilities provided by the AMC simulation software.

15.1 WHY A MODEL COMPUTER?

The choice of a model computer does need some justification, as some would argue that it is better to use a subset of an actual low level language. The arguments in favour of a model are generally as follows:

(1) A model computer enables an integrated treatment of the topics of Processor Architecture, Machine Language and Assembly Language to be given.
(2) The design of all three aspects can be pitched at an appropriate level for the capabilities of the students.
(3) It is possible to introduce essential concepts independent of any implementation constraints.
(4) The model computer can be representative of a range of actual computers, rather than being tied to a particular machine.

A considerable amount of research and development work is required in order to put these potential advantages into practice. The next few sections outline the main stages of this process.

15.2 DESIGN INFLUENCES; SYLLABUS, STUDENT CAPABILITIES AND REAL MACHINES

There have been three main influences on the design of the AMC, namely the requirements of 'A' Level syllabuses in this area, the architecture and low level languages of actual computers and the capabilities of typical 'A' Level students. These three influences are discussed in the next sections.

'A' Level Syllabus Requirements

The syllabuses of the six UK Examinations Boards currently offering Computing Science or Computer Studies at 'A' Level [2-7], differ in detail and emphasis in the areas of Processor Architecture and Low Level Languages, but they have sufficient common ground for a single design to be satisfactory for all of them. The principal topics in these areas identified by these Boards may be summarised as follows (topics in brackets are included in a minority of syllabuses):

PROCESSOR ARCHITECTURE
Control Unit
Addressing Concept of an address, addressing techniques, number of addresses, address modification: indexing and indirect addressing, use of a stack.

Instructions Concept of a stored instruction, instruction formats, instruction cycle, information flow during instruction execution, interrupts (instruction decoder).

Arithmetic and Logic Unit Accumulator(s), register(s), serial and parallel devices for processing data by operations on bit strings, (overflow and other indicators).

Main Store Addressable store, RAM (and ROM).

Input/Output Concept of input and output (buffers, busy signals from peripherals, DMA).

LOW LEVEL LANGUAGE FEATURES
Instructions Mnemonic codes, relationship between machine and assembly language, subprograms, (assembler directives, macros, parameter passing, recursive subprograms, use of stack).

Addressing Symbolic addressing, addressing modes: immediate, absolute, indirect, indexed, (relative).

Operations Fetch and store, logical, arithmetic, shift, branch, (skip, character handling) operations.

Input/Output Input and output instructions, (data conversion, flags and interrupts).

Student Capabilities

'A' Level students are generally of above average capability, and many have previous experience in computing. Nevertheless, the majority are newcomers when it comes to a fairly thorough introduction to Processor Architecture and Low Level Languages. Accordingly, it is essential that the design of a model computer satisfy a number of requirements, which are important in any educational material. These are:

Simplicity

The system must achieve its functional objectives in as simple a manner as possible. It has been pointed out a number of times [8, 9] that simplicity is an important requirement of the design of any system.

Consistency

It is important that various parts of the system behave in a consistent manner, and that special cases be avoided wherever possible.

Integrity

The various parts of the system must be seen to work together to form an integral unit. It must be possible to form an overall picture of the system which is the basis of a more detailed appreciation of various aspects.

Clarity of concept

It is important that the underlying design concepts of the system be clearly visible and as far as possible easily understandable.

These somewhat daunting requirements are the second area of influence on the AMC design. They also form a set of criteria against which the performance of the system can be measured.

The Design of Actual Computers

As a review of the whole range of computers currently available is quite impossible, a selection had to be made of as small representative subset. Selection criteria for the subset included that it span the whole range of processing power, that the selected machines be widely used and well regarded and that they reflect up-to-date ideas in processor architecture and low level language design. On the basis of these criteria, the following four machines [10-14] were chosen:

Z80 microprocessor
PDP-11 minicomputer
ICL 2900 Series mainframe computer
Cray 1 megacomputer.

Evaluation of these computers enabled a model computer architecture to be evolved which is broadly representative of actual computers and in theoretical processing power lies somewhere between the Z80 and the PDP-11, where, it is suspected, the 'centre of gravity' of computing lies at present.

15.3 ARCHITECTURE AND LANGUAGES OF THE MODEL PROCESSOR, AMC

The design considerations outlined in the previous three sections led to the evolution of the AMC architecture. The design went through several iterations, including parallel evolution and evaluation of two alternatives at one stage. The resulting processor is a 16 bit, single accumulator, one-address machine. Its register structure is shown in Fig. 15.1.

AMC Machine Language

AMC machine instructions consist of a 16 bit word optionally followed by a 16 bit address or **operand**. The instruction set is divided into groups, instructions within each group having the same format and performing related operations. For example there is a memory addressing group, a register manipulation group, a stack manipulation group, a (relative) branching group etc. Spreading the redundancy provided by 16 bit instructions in this way makes machine instructions easier to understand.

There are a few general rules relating to the format of all instructions:

bits 0 to 3   : group
bits 4 to 7   : instruction in group
bits 8 to 15 : depending on group, same format throughout group:
          For example, memory addressing group:
          bits 8 to 11   : register
          bits 12 to 15 : addressing mode.

Addressable registers are

1   Accumulator
2   Index Register
3   Stack Pointer

Addressing modes are

1   Immediate operand
2   Absolute Address
3   Indirect Address
4   Indexed Address

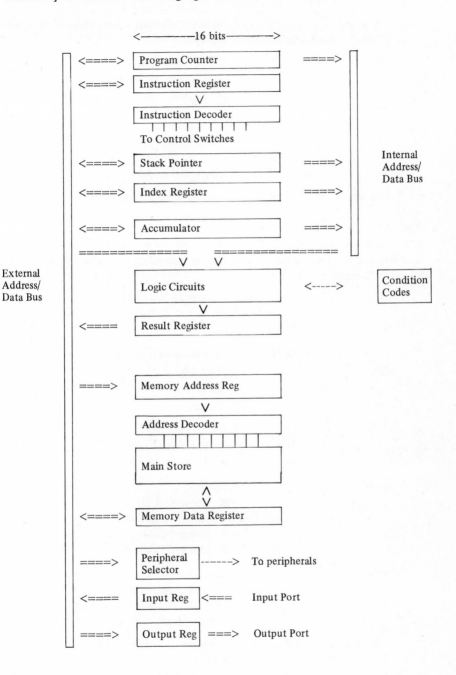

Fig. 15.1 – AMC Register Structure.

Subdividing the bits into sets of four enables machine instructions to be easily represented in hexadecimal notation. For example:

Machine Instruction	Meaning of Hex Digits	
1313 023A	Group 1	: Memory Addressing
	Instr 3	: Add
	Register 1	: Accumulator
	Addr Mode 3	: Indirect
	Operand	: 023A

Interpretation : Add number of address contained in location 023A to Accumulator, placing result in Accumulator.

In all there are 56 implemented AMC machine instructions.

AMC Assembly Language

AMC assembly language has the usual features of mnemonic operation codes, symbolic addresses and data representation as decimal integers or ASCII characters. There are three directives:

BTE   reserves a store location for a byte (8 bits) of data
WRD reserves two consecutive store locations for a word (16 bits) of data
END marks the end of a program.

The format of AMC assembly language instructions is as follows:

Label	3 characters
Mnemonic Op Code	3 characters
Register	1 character:

           A Accumulator
           I Index Register
           S Stack Pointer

Addressing Mode	1 character:

           N Immediate Operand
  (blank) Absolute Address
           I Indirect Address
           D Indexed Address

Operand	3 characters:

Symbolic Address or ASCII character(s) between delimiters for example, /*/ or Signed integer in range − 128 to + 127

The language is best introduced by means of a simple example. The routine shown below inputs a sequence of characters and stores them in consecutive locations of AMC memory. The end of the input is marked by the character *. The start address of the storage area is declared in the program.

PROGRAM

Instruction			*Interpretation*
PTR WRD		CHR	Address of first character, later of current character.
AGN IRQ	T		Signal terminal to load character into Input Register.
INP	A		Copy character from Input Register to Accumulator.
CPB	A N /*/		Compare character with end-of-input marker.
BZE		OUT	Branch if difference is zero to instruction labelled OUT.
STB	AI PTR		Store character at address in location PTR.
LOA	A PTR		Load address of current character to Accumulator.
INC	A		Add 1 to contents of Accumulator.
STO	A PTR		Store address of next character in location PTR.
BRN		AGN	Branch to instruction labelled AGN to input next character.
OUT HLT			Halt on exit from loop.
CHR BTE			Storage for first character.
END			End of program.

Notice that the program uses indirect addressing via a pointer which is incremented after each character has been input in order to store a sequence of characters.

15.4 THE AMC SIMULATION PACKAGE

The AMC Simulation package is a fairly sizeable item of software which brings the AMC into existence on a number of popular microcomputers. Facilities provided by the software include the following:

- Clear AMC registers, main store and assembly code workspace
- Enter assembly language program from the keyboard
- Edit assembly language program
- List all or part of assembly language program
- Assemble all or part of assembly language program
- Store program on disk file
- Retrieve program from disk file
- Load machine code into AMC main store
- Run machine code, in one of the following running modes:

> display input and output only
> display registers
> single step with register display

- Display registers or main store locations
- Alter registers or main store locations.

One important design feature of the system is that it is cumulative. All data retains its current value until it is changed. Thus it is possible to load part of a program from a file, append code from the keyboard, assemble portions of the program at a time, run the program to a breakpoint, examine and alter registers or store locations and then resume running from the breakpoint. The assembler locates and identifies all errors encountered.

Nelsons 'A' Level Computing Science Series
Full details of the AMC design as well as the AMC Simulation Software will shortly be available as part of the 'A' Level Computing Science series to be published by Thomas Nelson Limited. The series comprises:

- An Introduction to Computing Science
- Further Computer Programming in Basic (plus disk of example programs)
- AMC Simulation Package (text plus disk)

A hardware implementation of the AMC is also under development.

REFERENCES

[1] Cockett, W. A., *An analysis of widely used low-level languages designed for computer education,* Brunel University, 1978.
[2] JMB *Computing Science 'A' Level Syllabus.*
[3] London University *Computing Science 'A' Level Syllabus.*
[4] Welsh Joint Education Committee *Computing Science 'A' Level Syllabus.*
[5] AEB *Computing Science 'A' Level Syllabus.*
[6] University of Cambridge Local Examinations Syndicate *Computing Science 'A' Level Syllabus.*
[7] Oxford Delegacy of Local Examinations *Computing Science 'A' Level Syllabus.*
[8] Wirth, N., On the Design of Programming Languages, *Information Processing Magazine,* 1974.
[9] Hoare, C. A. R., *Hints on Programming Language Design,* Stanford Artificial Intelligence Laboratory, 1973.
[10] Mostek, *Microcomputer Components Data Book,* 1979.
[11] Harrison, N., A guided tour of the Z80, *Personal Computer World Magazine,* 1979.
[12] Gill, A., *Machine and Assembly Language Programming of the PDP-11,* Prentice-Hall, 1978.
[13] Buckle, J. K., *The ICL 2900 Series,* McMillan, 1978.
[14] *Cray 1 System Programmer's Manual.*

CHAPTER 16

The possibililities of using CAL on Business Education Council Courses

Adrian Woods, Polytechnic of North London, Holloway Road, London

---

Over the last few years a wind of change has swept through Business Education, initiated by the Business Education Council (BEC) [1]. *Among the many innovations the two most important are the interdisciplinary approach advocated and the widespread use of educational objectives in specifying curriculum content.*

Neither of these are new to teaching in general but certainly new to many teachers of Business Studies and have an impact on the way CAL may be developed within Business Studies. The BEC philosophy has not yet challenged degree or post graduate Business Studies: the remarks contained below do not relate to these levels but to the majority of non-degree level business studies courses run under the auspicies of BEC, and in particular to the Higher National Diploma in Business Studies. For many readers BEC is an unknown quantity, and before turning to how it affects the development of any CAL program I will first summarise some of its fundamental qualities.

16.1 INTERDISCIPLINARY NATURE OF BUSINESS EDUCATION AND COGNITIVE OBJECTIVES

BEC insists that the compulsory components of the course are not subject based. It says any course that is subject based will 'be viewed unfavourably by the Validation Committee, requiring re-submission of specifications modified to demonstrate a closer approach to the educational and vocational requirements of BEC's policies, [2]. To further strengthen the interdisciplinary nature of the course, cross-modular assignments (CMAs) are mandatory. CMAs function by linking compulsory units together in the form of assignments that the student has to pass to successfully complete the course.

The other innovation was the demand by BEC that teachers became more conscious of, and concerned with, educational objectives. Readers who are unaware of what this implies in terms of curriculum development can find a full explanation of the educational objectives employed by BEC in [3].

The effect of asking colleges to write submissions in terms of educational objectives meant that attention was focused on substantive knowledge to be transmitted and of the level this knowledge was to be taught. An example might clarify this important point. When designing courses for say a BA in Business Studies the syllabuses will contain material to be covered in terms of simple titles. If it is wished to have some teaching in Business Statistics the syllabus will list the material to be covered, that is,

Sources of Business Statistics
Collection and presentation of data
Measures of location and dispersion
Simple linear regression and correlation, etc.

Compare this to a BEC Syllabus and the difference in presentation is immediately apparent.

Identify the main sources of data external to an organisation including major official UK sources.

Collect sets of data relating to specified areas of business or economic activity.

Calculate and *use* appropriately measures of central tendency and standard deviation on data presented in different forms for business purposes.

Apply the concept of probability to typical business operation.

With the BEC courses a list of material is not sufficient, the *cognitive level*, indicated above the italic script, required has also to be specified. Furthermore, BEC insists that business education should be concerned with the student's activity, that is, not only what he knows, but what he can do (for example; apply, analyse, synthesise, evaluate).

These two changes, interdisciplinary subjects and educational objectives and their impact on CAL will be explored below. Often traditional methods of teaching and CAL have been preoccupied with knowledge and although this is part of any educational programme, BEC has to be supplemented by methods that give the students skills in terms of business. This implies broadly a two fold classification between cognitive objectives and skills objectives which is not the one normally found in the literature where perhaps either a three fold classification is often used; cognitive, affective and psychomotor, or teaching concentrates on only the cognitive domain.

The cognitive objectives asked for by BEC can be encompassed by Bloom's taxonomy: knowledge, comprehension, application, analysis, synthesis and evaluation. Skill objectives require more than reflection or thinking, they require actions. These actions are more than just manual dexterity as they include abilities associated with interpersonal skills, decision making and problem solving [4].

Given this proposed two fold classification the question arises as to which teaching strategies will be most successful in attaining the objectives to be realised?

16.2 TEACHING STRATEGIES

Davies [5] argues that for lower level cognitive objectives lectures, programmed learning and computer assisted instruction are best. This is broadly supported by Bligh [6] who suggests that at least for lectures lower level cognitive material can be realised but lectures do not in themselves promote thought. He claims that the principle objective of lectures is the acquisition of information by students.

For higher order cognitive skills Davies sees methods based on active student centred learning as being superior. Whereas group discussion is not as effective as lectures for low level cognitive objectives, it is far superior in realising higher order ones. He goes on further to stress the role case studies can play in the acquisition of these higher order objectives. Bligh, referring to an earlier study by Seigel [7] concludes that lectures do not require thinking from the students as do more active methods of instruction.

The other part of the proposed classification, objectives relating to skills, and how best to acquire them still needs some analysis. Clearly lectures are not a very effective way of acquiring skills as opposed to more active student participation. Mayo [8] argues that social skills, important in business and commerce, are best developed by practice, imitation and trial and error, that is by doing.

The implications are that lower level cognitive objectives are best taught by lectures and by computer assisted methods, whilst higher level cognitive ones require more active methods such as group discussion and role playing and that the skills required are best promoted by 'doing'.

Summary

Objectives	Teaching Strategy
Lowest level cognitive objectives	Lectures, programmed learning and CAL
Higher level cognitive objectives	Group discussion and case study,
Skills problem solving communications	Doing and practice.

The final part of the teaching strategy is that BEC emphasise that the compulsory units must be interdisciplinary and these units are to be assessed through cross modular assignments (CMA). The content of the CMAs includes both lower and higher cognitive objectives as well as skill objectives drawn from several disciplines.

16.3 CAL'S PLACE IN BUSINESS EDUCATION COUNCIL COURSES

What role can CAL play in this system? As Davies points out, programmed learning and computer assisted learning are effective in realising lower level cognitive skills. At the Polytechnic of North London we are in the process of preparing material on this to run on the Department of Business Studies' PETs. Getting material for these programs was relatively easy, as part of our existing assessment strategy includes multiple choice tests drawn from our BEC courses. Each question on the multiple choice paper relates back to a cognitive objective in our HND course.

The program consists of a series of questions with some probable answers and the student will be required to indicate the correct one. Correct responses will allow the students to get to the next question whilst a wrong answer is immediately corrected by the machine indicating to the student which the right answere is. The basic design philosophy involved in this follows that first proposed by Skinner [9], and best illustrated by Skinner and Holland, *The Analysis of Behaviour*. Although it is not always possible to make the correct answer demand more than a trivial response from the student in general the responses do advance the student's understanding.

A more tricky problem arises when the sequence of questions is considered. Usually with linear programming of this type individual questions are linked together by having some common content. This is easily achieved when working within one subject discipline, but as one of the changes BEC introduced was requiring subjects to be multidisciplinary, some of the joins between material are discontinuous. The student has to then switch from one traditional subject to another without any proper linkages between the subjects.

Given this problem, the use of multiple choice questions drawn from compulsory subjects, although perhaps involving a rather unimaginative use of CAL, provide a useful supplement to existing teaching. More adventurous uses of CAL within this structure are being developed.

The application of **Intrinsic or branching programs** as developed by Crowder [10] and others offers ways of formulating programs that develop the student's ability on different cognitive levels. Within these branching programs care has been taken not to lead the student too far off the main track.

Previous to the introduction of BEC requirements I had several developed programs in the field of statistics. By reworking these into the BEC framework it is possible to explore different cognitive levels within one subject. For example, in our compulsory module on the Acquisition and Control of Resources, there is the following section:

Use simple techniques for forecasting future outcomes in Business.

(1) Illustrate the need for forecasting in business and differentiate between types of information needed for short — medium — and long term planning.

(2) Use simple graphical methods to determine the relationships between two variables.
(3) Use moving averages to smooth data and identify trends in data.
(4) Interpret time series derived from business data.
(5) Derive forcasts by extrapolation of past data, and recognise the limitations of such forecasts.

The key cognitive objectives are the Illustrate, Use, Use, Interpret and Derive. I had an existing time series program running on the PET; what I am doing now is adding to it by using real data so that the students will start to achieve the stated objectives. Also within this module is a section relating to modelling business situations:

Develop a model of a business problem and interpret the solution of the model.

(1) Develop a model of a real business system, for example
 (a) a model illustrating the effects of changes in costs or quantities of resources or sales on cash flow and/or profit;
 (b) a forecast of future activities developed by extrapolation from past data;
 (c) a model of a stock control system;
 (d) a forecast of the cash flows associated with a proposed capital investment decision;
 (e) a forecast of differential costs and revenues associated with alternative courses of action (for example, make or buy).
(2) Use the model to solve a given problem, using a computer and suitable software packages where appropriate.
(3) Interpret the result of the model referred to in (2).
(4) Assess the effects on the solution if some of the data is inaccurate or missing.

Here there is obvious scope for the use of micros. As will be mentioned below. I have already completed a stores management simulation that has immediate applicability to this section.

16.4 USE OF CAL WITH CROSS MODULAR ASSIGNMENTS

Where CAL has most to offer is in cross modular assignments (CMAs). Firstly the assignments are interdisciplinary, secondly lower level cognitive objectives have mainly been covered within the normal lecture/seminar framework and high level objectives have not and thirdly the development of skills, such as interpersonal relations and problem solving, can be tackled. The most advanced CAL program I have at present is designed to be used for CMAs concerned with stores management techniques. Two separate programs run; one is a stores simulation and the second is a simple calculation program to aid the students in making decisions based on the simulation program. This CMA requires the student to develop certain mathematical skills associated with the economic order quantity (EOQ) and to appreciate the nature of a stochastic process on the EOQ. Elements of report writing are included to get the student to comment on the problems posed by the simulation. Interpersonal skills are encouraged as students tackle this exercise in groups and they are assessed on how well they cope as individuals within their group situation.

Another CMA based on industrial relations has up to now been generated without a computer by using look up tables to ascertain the next move in a complex industrial relations problem. With the help of the Industrial Relations lecturer most of this can be put onto a PET or a similar machine, thus reducing the time before the results of decisions are known. The interaction between groups via the computer in this problem ensures that higher level cognitive objectives are covered plus problem solving skills are encouraged and interpersonal skills are developed.

The last area is the use of business games on the CMA program. On a trial run in 1980 these proved to be extremely popular with students and staff. We have developed our own software in the form of a very simple exercise played against the machine. Students make decisions on planning production, marketing, price and new capital formation and the computer calculates sales, cost and profits.

We have also used, again with success, PETPLAN. One of the problems with any CMA program is the cohesion between one assignment and the next and it has been suggested that one way around this would be to base not one CMA on a business game but a whole session's worth of CMAs, thus ensuring continuity between one CMA and the next. PETPLAN may well, in the future, form the base for such a structure.

Another popular piece of software that still needs careful revision to work on our CMA program is a macro economics game. Students can certainly interact with the program successfully, making changes to key economic indicators to see the effect these changes have on other economic variables. The drawback is that the other skills that the CMAs should be developing are not present. The only skill in terms of BEC that is really being developed is that of problem solving, whereas in the business game, the industrial relations program and the stores stimulation communication skills and interpersonal skills are encouraged. It might be argued that these are also encouraged if the economic game is played by groups, but I have found that even in groups the roles students play are too artificial. In the other programs students soon take on the roles assigned as they seem to be fairly realistic. Asking students to be Chancellor of the Exchequer or Prime Minister is unfair and they do not really benefit from playing the role. Consequently, this has not been used on the CMA program but it has been used in our other teaching.

Summary

	Use of CAL
Low level cognitive objectives	Linear programming techniques using existing multiple choice questions.
Higher level cognitive objectives	Branching programs. Using the computer as a super calculator to give instant answers to aid students with the problems.
Cross modular assignments	Business games simulation.
Problem solving Personal skills Communication skills	

16.5 CONCLUSION

The innovation in Business Education introduced by BEC offers excellent opportunities to anyone interested in using CAL in business studies. I believe their greatest potential will be in CMAs where CAL techniques will be enormously helpful. The close specification of education objects also provides a detailed framework within which CAL may be explored.

For further details on the impact of BEC on business studies see:

Joyce, P. and Woods, A.   *Reflections on One Experience of Designing the Core Programme for Business Education Council (BEC) Higher level courses,* Business Education 1980.

Joyce, P. and Woods, A.   *The Evolution of BEC, from Objectives to Teaching Strategies and Assessment Methods,* Business Education 1981.

For details of the programs used at the Polytechnic of North London, see:

Woods, A.   Economic Order Quantity, *Personal Computing,* 1979.
Woods, A.   Stores Simulation, *Personal Computing,* 1980.
Woods, A.   Use of micros in Business Studies, *Educational Computing,* Nov. 1981.

REFERENCES

[1] Business Education Council, (1976), *First Policy Statement,* Mar.
[2] Business Education Council, BEC Higher National Award, *Illustrative Material on Core Studies,* p. 4.
[3] Bloom, B. S. (Ed.), (1956), *Taxonomy of Educational Objectives: The Classification of Educational Goals, Handbook 1: Cognitive Domain,* David McKay Co.

[4] Mayo, F., (1949), *The Social Problems of An Industrial Civilisation*, Routledge and Kegan Paul.

[5] Davies, I. K., (1971), *The Management of Learning*, McGraw Hill.

[6] Bligh, D. A., (1971), *Whats the use of Lectures?*, Penguin.

[7] Bligh, D. A., *ibid.*, p. 33.

[8] Mayo, E., *op cit.*, p.19.

[9] Skinner, B. F., (1961), Teaching Machines, *Scientific American*, Nov.

[10] A useful source book on all aspects of this approach is:
Lunsdaine, A. A. and Glasser, R. (Eds.)., *Teaching Machines and Programmed learning, A Source Book.*, N.E.A. Department of Audio-Visual Instruction, Washington.

CHAPTER 17

School administration without discs: how much can be done?

Ian Birnbaum, Ramsey Abbey School, Ramsey, Huntingdon, Cambridgeshire

---

It is often thought that to use the computer profitably and successfully in school administration a disc system is a necessity. However, with a tape operating system as reliable as the PET's, it is possible to do some quite sophisticated work without discs.

In this article, I shall first describe the sort of administrative applications for which a PET with cassette storage is used a Ramsey Abbey School. I shall then discuss more generally the types of application where one can do without discs, and those where discs become essential. Finally, I shall consider some important aspects of tape data file management on the PET which help to ensure reliable storage.

17.1 ADMINISTRATIVE PROGRAMS USED AT RAMSEY ABBEY SCHOOL

Ramsey Abbey is a 14-18 comprehensive school with an intake of about 280 pupils each year. The pupils come from one feeder school, which divides the pupils into four bands, North, East, West, South in order of ability.

Each pupil has to make six option choices, though the same range of choices are not open to all the bands. The PET is used to help with the option sorting. Ramsey Abbey does not organise itself using bands, but the banding is useful for analysing the options, and so the information is retained until the analysis is complete.

The first task is to input the pupils' names and their option choices, band by band, to output the data to tape and to out clash tables.

The work of keying in the data is performed by sixthformers, who volunteer to become members of a Computer Operators Group. They will not usually be programmers and most, but not all, will be typists. There are considerable educational advantages in using sixthformers for tasks like this, for not only do they get a taste of what computer operation is like, they also feel very much closer to the running of the school.

The Deputy Head who is in charge of timetabling will offer various option schemes which are tested by the computer, a list of unfitted pupils being output. Once the best scheme is chosen the Deputy Head will put pupils into groups in the most economical way, results being recorded on cards using a number code. Thus one pupil's code may be 52,7,15,29,31,44. Putting this into numerical order automatically puts it into option order. Also on the card is the pupil's new form in the school.

A tape will be created of code translations – so that 7 = PH2, 15 = BY3, etc. – and computer operators, working directly from the cards, will input the numerical codes and form for each pupil band by band. The program will translate this into symbolic code for each pupil and, combined with the original data tape (from which the names are extracted), tape data is output which contains name, option choices with group numbers, and form.

When all the bands have been processed, they are combined and put into overall alphabetical order, boys first, and output to a master tape. This master tape can then be used for printing out all the form and option lists. Using a special amending program, data can be edited, deleted or inserted and re-saved to tape, and new lists can be output as required through the two-year period (that is, until the end of the fifth form for each fourth year intake).

The master tape is also used to produce subject choices for each pupil in tabular form for use by the School's Examination Officer. It is also used to print out all of the Maths and English groups, set by set, and also to provide form teachers with information on setting. Finally, it is used in a program which allows the Deputy Head to plan school practical exams so that they mesh with written papers in the most economical way.

The computer is also used to help with the administration of the Sixth Form. Subject choices at 'O' and 'A' level and general subject choices are input, and a general purpose master tape is produced. From this lists of all kinds are compiled by the computer at various times of the year, amendments being very easy to make using the amendment program.

The minimum hardware configuration required for all this is a 16k PET, a cassette deck and a printer, though in practice we use a 32k PET most of the time.

17.2 PRINCIPLES IN ADMINISTRATIVE PROGRAM DESIGN

Certain general principles can be formulated from our experience with cassette-based administration. Firstly it is clear that a disc system becomes essential when one wishes to regularly access small parts of a large data base. For example, if one wished to use the computer to store the names, dates of birth and telephone numbers of pupils, *and* to access any particular one at any time, then cassette storage would be hopelessly slow. However, if one wished to print out lists from this data, the lists being used for access, then cassette storage is quite feasible.

In general, if many lists will be produced from the same data, it is important to be able to load the entire tape into memory first. Assuming about a 3000 byte program, with a record length of N characters, this allows about $3000/N$, $11000/N$ and $26000/N$ records with 8k, 16k and 32k of memory respectively. With a school of 280 pupils per year this allows a maximum record length of about 40 characters with a 16k machine. This is enough for all the programs discussed in the section above, but not for a names and addresses program which would require a 32k machine.

With larger data bases than about 100 characters per pupil for 280 pupils then again a disc system becomes essential. One can sometimes get over size limitations by processing data sequentially from tape, but it is not always possible (for example, alphabetical ordering) and it is prohibitively slow if many passes need to be made through the data (for example, when printing a complete set of subject lists).

The slowness of tape input as opposed to disc input is certainly a disadvantage. A general rule of thumb is to allow 30 seconds for each 1000 bytes of data. With the largest data base mentioned above, this means a 13 minute wait. Such a long wait is tolerable if the file has to be loaded and saved only a few times in a year. All of the administrative applications described above are like this and furthermore none requires a wait of more than about 5 minutes. The making and correcting of lists does not occur very often, and corrections can be 'saved up' until the time comes to reprocess the lists. Options-choosing and examinations only occur once a year. It follows that for relatively infrequent administrative tasks (though very important ones all the same) the penalty of slow loading is not a great burden.

There are two cases, then, where cassette storage is not viable: when there is a need to access randomly from a data base; and when there is a need to access all the items simultaneously from a data base larger than the available RAM.

However, many administrative applications in schools require neither of these, as the examples in the section above show. Indeed, it is arguable that problems of security on the one hand (if the computer and disc system are in a public area) and the waste of resources on the other (if the hardware is in a restricted-access office) severely limit the scope for random access of information in a school. In any case, since financial restrictions make cassette-based systems inevitable for many schools for the next few years, it is important to see how best we can use them in administration. And, in this regard, the PET is unrivalled. Let us see why.

17.3 RELIABILITY OF CASSETTE DATA STORAGE

The PET tape operating system with its digital pulse recording, checksum calculations and redundant storage is one of the most reliable on the market. It is worth expanding on this a little, since it will increase our confidence in storing important administrative information on a lowly cassette tape.

Each byte of data is recorded on tape as a series of pulses: a '0' is one short length pulse followed by a medium length pulse; a '1' is one medium followed by one short. After the eight bits are recorded, a checksum bit is encoded. This depends on the sum of the previous eight bits. Finally, a word marker bit (consisting of one long and one medium pulse) is encoded, to mark the end of a byte. This use of pulses has the great advantage of allowing for a considerable variation in recording and playback speed. Special firmware uses the ten-second leader which is put on the tape by the system, and which consists of short pulses, to synchronise the pulse timing. In this way, the PET performs an automatic read correction to the tape speed.

In data tape storage, as opposed to program storage, each character is encoded into ASCII. Thus the character A becomes 65, which is encoded on tape as 01000001.

Each time a program directs a string to tape, the string first goes in ASCII to a cassette buffer. Although the buffer is 192 bytes long, after the 191st byte is sent to the buffer, program operation stops while the buffer is emptied onto tape. Each byte on tape is followed by a checksum digit and word-marker. The whole block of 191 characters is recorded twice, the second identical block following the first; the reason for this 'redundant' storage will become clear in a moment. In order to allow the cassette deck to reach operating speed, both when writing and when reading back, the pair of blocks are preceded by 2 seconds of short pulses.

When data is read from tape, program execution is suspended while the data is put into the buffer. During this time, a check is made to see that the checksum bit corresponds to the sum of the preceding 8 bits; if it does not the byte is temporarily stored in another buffer (which has room for 31 such bytes) and is corrected by using the 'redundant' storage block. Hence audio dropouts, which affect some tape operating systems markedly, rarely present a problem to the PET. There are only two occasions when self-correction cannot take place: if exactly the same error has occurred in the redundant block as on the original block; or if more than 31 checksum errors occur in one block. These things happen so rarely that they are not worth worrying about.

Once the buffer is filled, INPUT# will fill the input buffer with bytes from the cassette buffer. Program executions will continue until the cassette buffer empties, and then the tape is turned on again for the next block of 191 bytes to be read in. By using this method, the acceleration and decleration delays caused by the cassette motor are relatively insignificant.

17.4 SOFTWARE TECHNIQUES WITH CASSETTE DATA STORAGE

There are a number of software ideas connected with data type files which make the writing of programs using cassette storage still more reliable.

(a) Naming files

It is useful to give a data file a name, but unfortunately the name is not returned when the file is read in a program. When you load a program by typing LOAD (or shift RUN/STOP) PET responds with the name of the program when it has found it; this does not happen automatically with data files.

However, there is a simple machine code routine which will do this. Here it is using a basic loader program:

```
10 FOR I = 826 TO 839
20 READ D : POKE I, D: NEXT I
30 DATA 162, 1, 189, 126, 2, 32, 210, 255
40 DATA 232, 224, 17, 208, 245, 96
```

Run this program once and then save the resulting machine code program from the monitor (it runs from $033A to $0347). You can then load it when required. (The routine allows a maximum name length of 16 characters. If you would like to use longer names, the 17 on line 40 may be changed to any number up to 188).

The following small subroutine used in conjunction with this machine code routine will produce the desired result (M$ should be given the value "LOADING" or "VERIFYING" depending on the function performed (see section (c) below)):

```
1000 OPEN 1: PRINT" <CD> FOUND "; : SYS 826 : PRINT M$
1010 RETURN
```

(b) Saving text

Some administrative tasks require the saving of text which might potentially contain commas or colons or which may have leading spaces. Attempts to subsequently read such text will result in errors, because the comma or colon will be understood as a text delimiter or the leading spaces will be lost. Thus if you wished to save 25, High Street and then recall it you would just get 25 for the comma would mark the end of the text. To get round this you need to save "25, High Street and this can be done by writing PRINT#1, CHR$(34)+A$ where A$ is the line of text to be saved.

Errors also occur if you save a field longer than 79 characters and attempt to INPUT # it. You can get round this by using GET #, but the best solution is to split up the record and to concatenate after input.

(c) Verifying files

Another useful aspect of program files is their easy verification: all that is necessary is to type VERIFY. Unfortunately, this is not available with data files, but if the data saved has been retained in an array, then it is possible to simulate the function in software. Here is the coding:

2000M$ = "VERIFYING" : GOSUB 1000
2010 FOR I = 1 TO N : INPUT#1, D$
2020 IF (ST = 64 AND I < > N) OR D$ < > A$(I) THEN M$ =
                              "ERROR" : GOTO 2040
2030 NEXT I : M$ = "OK"
2040 CLOSE 1 : PRINT " <CD> VERIFYING " M$
2050 RETURN
(GOSUB 1000 refers to the program in section (a)).

This subroutine should be called immediately after the data has been saved. A suitable message like 'Ready to verify now. Rewind tape. Press 'space' when ready' should be output first, of course. When returned from the subroutine, check the value of M$. If M$ = "ERROR", direct the program back to the save routine and try again.

Finally, it is worth remarking that even with all these checks on reliability you should still keep two copies of every data file, stored in different places. It has been known for a stray magnetic field. . . . .

CONCLUSION

The PET has a very reliable tape operating system which with software embellishments can be made virtually error-free. Thus cassette storage provides a cheap and efficient way to achieve computerised administration in a school for important though relatively rare tasks. Only if regular random access is required or if the data base is very large will a disc system be necessary.

Addresses of Contributors

Roy Atherton
  Bulmershe College of Higher Education
  Bulmershe, Earley, Reading RG6 1HY

Peter Avis
  The Anthony Gell School
  Wirksworth, Derbyshire DE4 4DX

Annette Barnard
  Department of Educational Enquiry
  The University of Aston in Birmingham, Gosta Green, Birmingham B4 7ET

Ian Birnbaum
  Ramsey Abbey School
  Ramsey, Huntingdon, Cambridgeshire PE17 1DH

Peter Bishop
  Logica VTS Limited, 64 Newman Street, London WIA 4SE

David Burghes
  School of Education
  The University of Exeter, St. Lukes, Exeter EX1 2LU

Borge Christensen
  Viben 34, Tonder DK6270, Denmark

Danny Doyle
  9 Main Street, Gawcott, Bucks

Richard Fothergill
  Cheriot House, Coach Lane Campus, Newcastle upon Tyne NE7 7XA

Peter Goodyear
Department of Educational Enquiry
The University of Aston in Birmingham, Gosta Green, Birmingham B4 7ET

Nick Green
Commodore Business Machines (UK) Limited
675 Ajax Avenue, Trading Estate, Slough, Berkshire SL1 4BD

Kathleen Hennessey
Department of Computation
The University of Manchester Institute of Science and Technology
PO Box 88, Manchester, M60 1QD

Bob Lewis
S. Martin's College, Bowerham Road, Lancaster MA1 3JD

Adrian Oldknow
West Sussex Institute of Higher Education
Upper Bognor Road, Bognor Regis, Sussex PO21 1HR

Christopher Smith
Department of Physiology
Queen Elizabeth College, University of London
Campden Hill Road, London W8 7AH

Keith Tomlinson
Computer Division, City of Bradford Metropolitan Council
Britannia House, Bradford, West Yorkshire BD1 1HX

David Walker
Director, Scottish Microelectronics Development Programme
Dowanhill, 74 Victoria Crescent Road, Glasgow G12 9JN

David Williams
Department of Biochemistry
Brunel University, Uxbridge, Middlesex UB8 3PH

Adrian Woods
Department of Business Studies
Polytechnic of North London, Holloway Road, London N7 8DB

Glossary

AMC	— A-level model computer.
ASCII	— American Standard Code for Information Interchange.
BASIC	— Beginner's All-purpose Symbolic Instruction Code.
BEC	— Business Education Council.
CAD	— Computer Assisted Design.
CAE	— Computer Assisted Experimentation.
CAI	— Computer Assisted Instruction.
CAL	— Computer Assisted Learning.
CAS	— Computer Assisted Simulation.
CET	— Council for Educational Technology.
CMA	— Cross Modular Assignments.
COMAL	— Common Algorithmic Language.
MEP	— Microelectronics Education Programme.
MUSE	— User's group, originally called Minicomputer users in Secondary Education.
NCC	— National Computer Corporation.
PETMAS	— PET Multiple Access System.
PETNET	— PET network using public telephones.

Index